WILL HOBBS

BEARSTONE

 HAMPTON-BROWN

THE EXCHANGE

Can people
change on their own,
or do they need others?

On-Page Coach™ (introductions, questions, on-page glossaries), The Exchange, back cover summary © Hampton-Brown.

Hampton-Brown
P.O. Box 223220
Carmel, California 93922
800-333-3510
www.hampton-brown.com

Printed in the United States of America

ISBN-13: 978-0-7362-2810-7
ISBN-10: 0-7362-2810-1

06 07 08 09 10 11 12 13 14 10 9 8 7 6 5 4 3 2

For Jean

**With special thanks to Greg, Ed, Dad, Joe, Dan, Jeff, Jean, Diane,
Matt, Suzy, and Pepsi for all the Pine River memories.
Thanks to Loyd for the inspiration and to Mike for the story
of his ride through the Window.**

Cloyd runs away from a group home to look for his father. He is shocked by what he finds.

1

Cloyd stood a step from the door of the hospital room. His father was in that room. "Are you sure you have to see him in person to deliver those flowers?" the nurse asked.

"They won't pay me unless I **deliver them in person**."

Cloyd didn't think it would work if he told her who he was. He had **run away from the Ute group home** in Colorado and **hitched** all the way to Window Rock, Arizona, to find his father. That's where the Navajos kept the records about everyone in the whole tribe, and there he found out that yes, there was a Leeno Atcitty, and his address was listed as the Indian Health Service Hospital in Window Rock. He was a patient there.

Cloyd wondered how he might get into his father's

....

deliver them in person give the flowers to the patient

run away from the Ute group home left a place for Native American boys who have problems at home

hitched asked strangers to drive him

hospital room to see him. If he told them who he was, there would be trouble because he had run away. Then he had an idea. He used the last of his money to buy some flowers.

For years Cloyd had been asking every Navajo he **happened to meet** if they knew a man named Leeno Atcitty. "What does he look like?" they'd ask. Cloyd couldn't tell them; he'd never known his father. He'd grown up without him, with only his sister and his grandmother. Cloyd knew just two things about his father—he was a Navajo, and he had disappeared after Cloyd was born. Nobody had seen him since.

When Cloyd was little, he used to talk to his sister about how badly he wanted to find his father, but she didn't seem to need to know him at all, so he **had kept his dream inside**. In the year since he'd been sent away, the more lonely he became, the stronger his desire grew to find his father. Now here he was with his heart pounding, following the nurse down the long hallway to his father's room.

The nurse **stopped short of the door** and said, "Why

....

happened to meet met

had kept his dream inside did not tell anyone his dream that he wanted to meet his father

stopped short of the door stopped outside the door

don't you let me take the flowers in."

Cloyd didn't know if this was going to work. He wasn't a good liar. He said, "I'm supposed to deliver them myself."

"I've never seen you here before. Who did you say you're working for?"

He knew he had to do something quick. Like a rabbit in the sagebrush, Cloyd was into the room.

What he saw terrified him. This wasn't even a human being. It was more like a shriveled-up mummy attached to a bunch of tubes. One went into his nose and one went into his arm. A third came out from under the sheet. How could this be his father? Was it even alive? "What's **the matter** with him?" he asked as evenly as he could.

"Have you ever heard of the expression 'brain dead'? It means his heart and his lungs still work, but his brain is . . . well, dead. I tried to tell you, it's **not a pretty sight**. He won't know about the flowers."

Cloyd had to keep talking, or the nurse would **get onto him**. He had to put away his terror, not show any emotion on his face. He was good at that. "How did this happen?"

....

the matter wrong

not a pretty sight hard to look at him

get onto him figure out he was not a real delivery person

7

"Car accident," she said. "I don't know any details."

"How long has he been like this?"

"Four years."

"Are you sure he's Leeno Atcitty?"

"Yes, of course."

"Where's he from?"

"I think I heard that once . . . Utah, I think. Monument Valley. I wonder if this could be the man you were looking for. Nobody ever sent him flowers before."

He knew it was his father. His father came from Monument Valley. Besides, the Navajos listed only one Leeno Atcitty.

Cloyd shrugged. "The people that ordered the flowers said he had a broken leg. Is there another Leeno Atcitty in the hospital?"

He sneaked one last look at his father. **The terror returned full force.** How could this . . . **wrinkled, shrunken shell of a human being** be his father? He forgot to wait for her reply. He turned and left without

....

The terror returned full force. He was scared again.

wrinkled, shrunken, shell of a human being small, old body

looking back.

"No," she said after him. "I'm sure there isn't. . . . There must have been some mistake."

He threw the flowers in the trash.

BEFORE YOU MOVE ON...

1. **Plot** Why did Cloyd pretend to deliver flowers to the hospital?

2. **Inference** Why did Cloyd want to find his father? What were his hopes?

LOOK AHEAD Cloyd's dream of meeting his father ended. Read pages 10–17 to find out what he does next.

Cloyd lives in a group home for Native American boys. He wants to go home, but his housemother wants him to live with an old rancher named Walter.

2

Cloyd wanted to go home to Utah, back to White Mesa. Every mile took him farther into Colorado, farther even than Durango, where he'd spent the lonely winter in the group home. He was looking out the window of the van at the beaver dams in the **creek** along the highway. There weren't any beaver dams where he came from.

His housemother didn't speak, and he was glad. She'd said it all before. How he couldn't go home for the summer, how she'd had this idea to put him on a ranch with an old man whose wife had died, and how much he was going to like it.

What was the old man going to be like? Cloyd wished he didn't have to meet this Walter Landis. Why wouldn't these people just leave him alone? All winter in the group

....

creek small river

His housemother The woman who took care of him at the group home

home, through the miserable days in school, he had **looked forward to** going home for the summer. Now even that was being taken away from him. They were afraid his grandmother wouldn't make him **mind**, that she'd let him disappear into the canyons again. Cloyd thought about how good that would be, to disappear and be free. He wanted to run away again, hitchhike home to White Mesa. When he was trying to find his father, he'd hitched all over.

"Getting close," his housemother announced cheerfully. She pulled off the highway onto a bumpy dirt road. "Look, there's the river, Cloyd—the Piedra River—through the trees!"

Cloyd had already noticed the river and the big pines. It was so different from the high desert back home. He rolled the window down all the way. It smelled like . . . pine cones.

"**Walter's is** the only place north of the highway," Susan James said. "After his place, it's all wilderness for a hundred miles and more."

Cloyd noticed how she drove slowly and **deliberately**

....

looked forward to been excited about
mind behave; follow the rules
Walter's is Walter's home, or ranch, is
deliberately carefully

through the potholes, slower than she would have had to. There was only a short time left before she dropped him off. Probably she was going to tell him to behave. This rancher was an old friend of hers. There, ahead, was the gate. Cloyd thought how much he didn't want to meet this stranger. He could hide and then hitch to Utah. He could visit his grandmother, at night when nobody would know. Then he would **take off for** the canyons. Nobody could find him in the canyons.

"Would you open the gate, Cloyd? Just look at that lovely **orchard**."

He got out of the van and opened the gate. Through the orchard he could see open fields, sheds, and a barn. Mostly hidden behind two blue spruce trees stood a gray two-story house. Somebody's home, not his. He could see a small **figure** stepping off the porch. Susan James was driving through the gate. Cloyd was supposed to close it behind her. He did, and then he **bolted** into the trees.

"Cloyd!" she called. "Cloyd, you come back here right now!"

He ran quickly and quietly. She was chasing him.

....

take off for go to
orchard group of fruit trees
figure person
bolted ran quickly

Cloyd **darted this way and that**, then hid behind an enormous **boulder**. His heart was beating fast. He grinned; he knew she couldn't catch him. "For crying out loud," he heard her say.

Cloyd **skittered** twenty or more feet up the boulder's sloping backside, gained its nearly flat top, and lay on his belly. He heard her tramping around in the orchard and calling with her voice raised, thinking he was long gone. She was on her way back to the van when she and the old man met, not very far from the boulder. Cloyd could hear everything they said.

"So he's run off, has he, Susan?" the old man said. "And **here I ain't** even met him yet."

The voice sounded very old and very tired. Cloyd peeked over the edge and saw them talking. The old man's hands were in the pockets of his striped overalls, his shoulders were slumped, his bald head bowed. Purple veins stood out on his skull. The most surprising thing about him was his size. He was little. I'm taller and bigger than he is, Cloyd realized.

"Does he do that often—run away?" the old man asked.

....

darted this way and that ran one way, then turned and ran another way

boulder rock

skittered climbed quickly

here I ain't I have not

13

"Only once before, and it sure got him in a whole lot of trouble. . . . I just thought being out here and working with you might be good for him. A chance with school out to get away from the group home where he's been getting into so much trouble. School has been a disaster for him."

"Oh? Well, I wasn't so good at school myself. . . ."

Cloyd saw his housemother frown. "I'll bet this is a lot worse than you ever did, Walter. He failed all seven of his classes. The school says he just won't do the work, but I'm not sure he even knows how. He's fourteen, but he missed four years of school back in Utah."

"Four years! Where was he?"

"Out in the canyons, **herding** his grandmother's goats. I think he's at least half-wild."

The old man **grinned mischievously. "Now, ain't that somethin'."**

Cloyd liked the old man's **chuckle**. The rancher didn't act like other grown-ups.

"So he was living with his grandmother?" Walter asked. "What about his parents—why isn't he with them?"

"His mother's dead—died when he was born. She was

....

herding taking care of
grinned mischievously smiled in a playful way
"Now ain't that somethin'." "That's very interesting."
chuckle laugh

14

Ute. No one seems to know much about his father, just that he's a Navajo. He left when she died. Cloyd's always lived with his mother's people. So tell me about yourself, Walter. How've you been doing?"

"**Not worth a darn.** Since Maude **passed away** and I sold off the cows, I haven't even **put up a hay crop**."

"But look at these beautiful peaches," Susan James said brightly. "You can't tell me you're not taking care of this peach orchard."

It's for her, Susan . . . for Maude. You know how she loved the peaches."

Cloyd peered into the thick green foliage. Until now, he hadn't noticed the trees around the boulder, he'd been **so intent on listening**. He was astonished. He never knew peach trees could grow so large, so full and lush, or **set** so much fruit. Peaches were treasured at White Mesa. He had always helped his grandmother harvest them, and it was a special time. But her trees couldn't begin to compare with these. He admired the rancher for owning these trees.

"Just look at all those baby peaches," Susan James said, pointing to branches loaded with fruit. "It amazes me

....

Not worth a darn. Not very well.

passed away died

put up a hay crop planted hay

so intent on listening listening so carefully

set grow

15

that you can raise them here at all. I've never seen peaches **at this altitude**, much less in a canyon. Doesn't the cold air **settle**?"

The old man had that **impish** grin on his face again. "That's what makes it interesting."

"Do you still have that gold mine you always talked about? With the price of gold going up every day, you must be getting ideas."

The rancher sighed. "Oh, I've still got the Pride of the West, an' I still believe in **her** as much as ever, but I'm not so sure as I used to be that I'll ever get back there."

Cloyd turned onto his back and studied the cliffs high on the mountain above the river canyon. In reds and whites, the cliffs seemed like a huge chunk of the desert hovering over the forests. They reminded him of home. In a moment, he realized that the boulder underneath him made a perfect fit with a huge notch in the cliffs up above. It must have fallen long ago, leaving behind a shallow cave. He felt good about his **insight**. He wasn't stupid, like

....

at this altitude this high up in the mountains
settle make it hard to grow peaches
impish playful
her the mine
insight understanding of what happened

they thought. It was the first of June, **a brilliant turquoise day**, and he was out of school at last. He kind of liked the old rancher, too. I can hitchhike to Utah later, he thought. Anytime.

Sliding off the rock, Cloyd slipped through the orchard and vanished among the tall trees, then began to climb. He didn't know he was climbing toward a treasure and **a turning point**. He wanted only to reach that piece of desert in the sky.

....

a brilliant turquoise day a day with a bright, bluish green sky
a turning point something that would change his life

BEFORE YOU MOVE ON...

1. **Character** Reread pages 10–11. What did Cloyd want?

2. **Character's Motive** Reread page 17. Why did Cloyd decide to stay at Walter's farm? Give two reasons.

LOOK AHEAD Read pages 18–26 to find out what treasures Cloyd finds in the cliffs.

Cloyd climbs a cliff and goes into a cave.
There he finds some secret treasures of the
ancient Native American people.

3

Under the cover of the big pines, Cloyd climbed the steep slope in leaps. As he climbed, the ranch buildings shrank until only their shiny metal roofs showed, and the peach orchard looked like a bright green circle with a sandy center. A herd of horses appeared in a **pasture** by the river. He was pleased to see that the old man had horses. He used to have a horse once.

Cloyd **let his thoughts take him back to White Mesa, as they had** all winter. Almost a year away from his grandmother and his sister, he'd had to live at White Mesa in his mind or **wither away and become nobody**. All winter in Durango as Cloyd sat in one classroom, then passed like a sleepwalker at the bell to the next, his spirit

....

pasture field

let his thoughts take him back to White Mesa, as they had thought about White Mesa, which he had thought about

wither away and become nobody forget who he was

roamed the canyons with the flock. He **put out of his mind now** his other dream, the one he used to live for, the one that had turned into the man in the hospital bed in Window Rock. White Mesa was his whole world now.

Finally he stood atop the red-and-white sandstone cliffs. They had the same feel as the cliffs in the canyons where he used to take the goats. But he'd never seen a view like this one. This was a shining new world. To the north and east, peaks still covered with snow shone in the cloudless blue sky. He'd never seen mountains so sharp and rugged, so fierce and splendid. Below him, an eagle soared high above the old man's field. **It was a good sign.**

Then he remembered his grandmother's parting words as he left for Colorado. She told him something he'd never heard before: their band of Weminuche Utes hadn't always lived at White Mesa. Colorado, especially the mountains above Durango, had been their home until gold was discovered there and the white men wanted them **out of the way**. Summers the people used to hunt and fish in the high mountains, she'd said; they knew every stream, places so **out of the way** that white men still hadn't seen

....

put out of his mind now stopped thinking about
It was a good sign. It made him feel hopeful.
out of the way to leave
out of the way hard to find

them. "So don't feel bad about going to Durango," she told him.

Cloyd **regarded the distant peaks** with new strength, a fierce kind of pride he'd never felt before. These were the mountains where his people used to live. Maybe he should stay at the ranch. Maybe he could follow the river all the way up to those peaks and stand atop the highest one. If he worked hard, there would be time off. Maybe the old man would let him take one of his horses.

Tucked under a high ridge, the **outcrop suddenly lost the sun**. He should be returning to the ranch. He wondered if his housemother had driven back to Durango with his duffel bag. Halfway down the side of the cliffs, he discovered a ledge that might lead across them. That's what he liked to do back in the canyon country: follow ledges across cliffs. You never knew what you might find. This one led to that shadowy cave, the notch he'd seen from the orchard. Its high, arching roof was indeed the perfect match to the backside of the boulder he'd climbed among the peach trees.

Cloyd **sprang** to the ledge. If he was careful, he could

....

regarded the distant peaks looked at the mountain tops

outcrop suddenly lost the sun land sticking out stopped being covered with sunlight

sprang jumped

follow it, at least for a way. Below him the cliff fell more than a hundred feet. There was no good reason he had to get to the cave, yet he knew he would try it. The place itself **was driving him on**. The cliff houses in the canyons used to **exert the same pull on him**. He'd managed those climbs, nearly as difficult as this one, by using the natural cracks in the canyon walls and the handholds the **Ancient Ones** had carved. And he'd stood many times in their ancient homes like nests, which were said to be unreachable without ladders. When he reached those places, he felt good, standing alone in a good place.

The ledge narrowed to a seam. Arms spread wide, fingers splayed on the sandstone, Cloyd started across it with his face to the cliff wall. Carefully he edged sideways on the tips of his toes with his right foot gingerly exploring, then choosing new footing, the left following after, until he was nearly there. **With a swoon** he realized he could no longer lean into the cliff. The shape of the rock had forced his body weight out over thin air, and he was in bad trouble. Stretched tight, the tendons above his heels began to quiver, then to tremble. His strength

---

was driving him on   made him want to climb
exert the same pull on him   make him feel the same way
Ancient Ones   Native Americans who lived a long time ago
With a swoon   Almost fainting

deserted him in a rush. He paused to rest, but his legs began to shake violently.

His fingers started to go numb. He fought the panic and tried to think. He knew he had to go forward, reach the cave, and rest. He'd never make it back unless he could rest.

Cloyd breathed deeply and **summoned a little strength into his legs**. He started out again, more quickly than before. Shuffling the last few steps, he fell gasping onto the chalky floor of the cave.

Once he **caught his breath**, Cloyd looked for what he might find. It would take his mind off the return across the cliff. If this cave were back in the canyon country, he thought, it would have **a ruin** in it and maybe some picture writing. But it was bowl-smooth and empty, except for a large **fin** of sandstone broken loose from the wall and ceiling. He noticed something wedged between the wall and the fin—a shape that didn't look quite natural. He shimmied into the dark, narrow crack until his hands closed on some kind of a bundle, and then he backed out into the light to see what it was.

....

summoned a little strength into his legs got ready to move again

caught his breath felt less tired

a ruin old objects

fin piece

He knelt and examined it up close. He probed with his fingers. Turkey feathers and fur, probably rabbit: hundreds of tiny bits of feather and fur wrapped around cords of yucca fiber. A blanket, a whole blanket in the style of the Ancient Ones.

Carefully he folded the blanket back and gasped to see a very small human face with empty eye sockets. The brown skin and black hair were still intact. At once he knew he was holding a **burial** in his hands, one of the Ancient Ones. His grandmother talked about such things, but he'd never seen one in all his time in the canyons. **Her advice came to mind**: behave carefully, treat the buried one with the utmost respect, and don't make any mistakes. The Ancient Ones are **not people to be trifled with**.

An infant, he realized. Buried in the position his grandmother had described, with the legs folded and tucked against the stomach. The best thing to do was think a good **intention** and return it to its resting place.

When Cloyd wriggled back with the bundle to the place where he'd found it, he saw the silhouette of a piece

....

burial a body that had been buried
Her advice came to mind He remembered what she told him
not people to be trifled with people to respect and honor
intention thought

of pottery, a jar with handles and a short, slender neck. He brought it into the open where he could see it, and **took in** its beauty and wholeness. Before this he'd found countless **shards** with similar black-lined designs, but never anything close to a whole pot. It was said they were worth a thousand dollars unbroken.

As he turned the pot on its side to admire it, something moved inside. He let the loose object fall gently into his hand. **His heart leaped** to see a small blue stone about two inches long, worn smooth by long handling. Turquoise. Two eyes, a snout, and a humped back. A bear. Surely, a bear to accompany the infant on the long journey.

His grandmother had told him about bears. The most important of all animals to the Utes, she'd said—friend and relative of man, bringer of strength and luck. If you could make a bear your personal **guardian**, you would be a strong man and lucky. In the old days, she said, when the people lived side by side with the bears, they would not kill them. That would **bring on themselves** the worst of bad luck.

....

took in looked at
shards pieces of pottery
His heart leaped He was excited
guardian protector
bring on themselves make them have

Cloyd turned the smooth blue stone in his hand. He felt he was meant to cross the cliff and find this stone. He had earned this bear-stone; his grandmother would understand. She was the only person he knew who remembered **the old ways** and believed in their power. He'd always wondered **if there was anything to her tales**. Now he was sure there was. With this **token**, he felt like a new and powerful person.

His grandmother had said that in the old days, people had a secret name that was known only to one other person—a name that described who they really were, not who the world thought they were. He had thought he would like to have such a name for himself, but this naming was no longer done. "I'll take a name for myself," he thought, **eyeing** the stone in his hand. "I don't need a father; I don't need anyone." Then he said aloud, "My name is Lone Bear."

Cloyd returned the jar to the Ancient One. He tried to talk to the infant in his mind, told it that it must have reached its destination by now, and please, he'd like to have the stone on his own life's journey because he, Lone

....

the old ways the things people did in the past
if there was anything to her tales if her stories were true
token treasure
eyeing looking at

Bear, had great need of the strength and good luck it would bring.

Cloyd put the smooth stone in his pocket and started back across the **precipice**. This time his legs did not shake. His feet were sure, and his fingers exerted a powerful grip on the face of the cliff.

He raced down the mountain in the twilight, **slowing his descent by clinging** for moments to branches as he flew by them. With the bear in his pocket, he wasn't afraid of the oncoming darkness. In an odd sort of way, he was looking forward to seeing the curious old man at the ranch. Maybe the summer job wouldn't be so bad after all. Maybe he could follow the river to the high peaks.

At any rate, he had the bearstone. He kept checking his pocket to make sure it was still there.

....

precipice ledge
slowing his descent by clinging slowing down by reaching out
At any rate No matter what happened

BEFORE YOU MOVE ON...

1. **Conclusions** Cloyd found a burial, a jar, and the bearstone. Why was the bearstone especially important to him?

2. **Character** Reread page 20. How was Cloyd different when he was in the mountains?

LOOK AHEAD Read pages 27–33 to find out what kind of person Walter is.

Cloyd meets Walter and learns more about the farm.
Cloyd thinks that the farm might be a good home.

4

It was dark. Walter tried to read his latest *Mining Gazette* in the parlor but couldn't concentrate **for worrying** about the teenager. He might've run off, but he might've slipped into the river. Swift and cold, the Piedra had drowned more than a few. He went outside, called the boy's name, and listened, but all he could hear was the river. Before too long he'd have to phone Susan James. He was supposed to call if Cloyd didn't **show up**.

Walter went inside and turned the heat down on the breaded pork chops he'd fixed. Since his wife died, he hadn't eaten regular meals. He'd eat a little of this and that, mostly from the canned goods in the basement. **Old friends who dropped by would admonish him for not keeping up his strength**, but as he told them, he was never

---

for worrying because he was worried

show up come to the house

Old friends who dropped by would admonish him for not keeping up his strength Friends who visited him told him that he should eat better

hungry. With the boy coming, he'd had to get into town, do some shopping, plan some meals, and start thinking about how to cook them.

He thought he'd take his flashlight downstream and look along the riverbank. In the mudroom closet Walter collected his wool coat and sat down on the bench to pull on his rubber boots. Two soft knocks sounded on the door. "Come on in," he said.

The boy stepped inside, avoiding Walter's eyes. Walter noticed the jeans first, wet from the knees down, then the fresh mud on the sneakers. The boy had gotten wet only minutes before, and not in the river. Crossing the **irrigation ditch**, Walter realized. Then he saw the T-shirt, with a fishhook-shaped rip across the belly. The shirt was **badly soiled**, yet white enough to accent the darkness of Cloyd's face and arms, which were the deepest shade of brown. His limbs were rounded, undefined, and he was chunky overall in the way of Ute men. Shiny black hair hung straight to his shoulders. Cloyd's large, round face **was devoid of expression**, unless it was the mouth **turning dourly down at the corners**. A bloody scratch

....

irrigation ditch long hole that carried water to the field
badly soiled very dirty
was devoid of expression did not show any feeling
turning dourly down at the corners frowning

shone bright red against his dark brown cheek.

"Got some supper here," Walter said. "You like pork chops?"

Cloyd shrugged. "Okay, I guess."

Walter put away the coat and flashlight, thinking **he'd best not** embarrass the boy by mentioning his clothes or the scratches. But he wouldn't have the boy tracking through the house in muddy sneakers. "I like to leave my outside shoes here in this mudroom," he said over his shoulder as he left.

Cloyd joined him in the kitchen in wet socks. "I put your stuff up in your room," Walter said. "That's upstairs. The stairs are just off the parlor, and the bathroom is off the backside of the kitchen—that closed door over there. Would you like to shower and change clothes, or eat right away?"

"I'm hungry," Cloyd said softly.

Walter caught the black eyes **darting** toward him, then quickly away. "That'd be fine. **Why**, I'm hungry myself."

They ate quietly. Cloyd liked that. The old man **wasn't all over him with questions**. He looked around.

....

he'd best not he should not

darting looking

Why I think

wasn't all over him with questions did not ask too many questions

The old man had an old-fashioned cookstove alongside the modern one. The cookstove was much like his grandmother's, only this one had bright blue enamel, where hers was all black and rusted in places. "You like that kind of stove?" he asked suddenly, pointing with a twist of the lips, as he finished up the food on his plate.

"Sure do. Still cook on it some, but mostly we used it for heating this side of the house in the winter. You can't beat them old stoves. **Say, whyn't you have another go-round?**" he said, indicating the pork chops and potatoes left on the platter. "Help yourself."

Cloyd shook his head. He felt freer refusing food.

"No? Make a good snack for tomorrow, then. But **hang on**. I've got something special to bring up from the basement for dessert."

On the old man's return, Cloyd sneaked a look at him. He sure was little. And he was really happy about his peaches—he had a big smile on his face and he carried the quart jar like it was a treasure.

"Like some?" Walter said with his grin.

Cloyd wasn't going to refuse this time; he nodded

....

Say, whyn't you have another go-round? Would you like more food?

hang on wait

enthusiastically. These peaches were large as store-bought. He loved peaches. He allowed the old man to dish up two large scoops of vanilla ice cream with the fruit.

The old man dished himself up some peaches and joined him.

"We have peaches at home, too," Cloyd said. "Not as big as yours."

"Size don't matter. That's pretty country, Utah is. Any canyons where you come from?"

"All over," Cloyd said. "Lots of ruins . . . from the Ancient Ones."

"**Cliff dwellers?** Like at Mesa Verde? Now ain't that somethin'."

Cloyd was curious. He had to ask. "Any ruins around here?" he asked carefully.

"Well, up on Chimney Rock Mesa, down the river a few miles and up the other side."

"I mean real close."

"Well, they say they lived all along the river—I've found a few grinding stones and **whatnot**, a few arrowheads and some **potsherds**. . . ."

....

Cliff dwellers? People who lived in caves on the cliffs?
whatnot other things like that
potsherds pieces of pottery

Cloyd felt the stone in his pocket. He almost wanted to tell, but he knew he shouldn't. It was his secret. It had to do with his secret name.

"So you had a look around today, did you . . . Cloyd?" the old man asked awkwardly.

Cloyd wanted to tell at least some of the truth. "I climbed up above the cliff," he said.

Walter **perked up**. "Why, that's one of my favorite places around the farm. I used to climb up there myself. Haven't for a **good while**, though."

"How come you call it a *farm*? This place is a *ranch*."

"Well, my wife **came from farm country** in Missouri, and she always said a ranch was like a house, but a farm was a home."

Cloyd finished the last of the syrup from the jar. He wasn't hungry anymore.

As he went upstairs, Cloyd noticed the picture of the old man's wife. It was on top of the bookcase by the stairs. He tried to imagine the white-haired woman with the friendly smile saying to the old man, "A ranch is like a house, but a farm is a home." He thought about what it

....

perked up looked interested
good while long time
came from farm country grew up on a farm

meant as he looked around his room, unpacked his things from his duffel bag, then lay down on the bed with the bearstone in the palm of his hand. This was a good place, Walter's farm.

BEFORE YOU MOVE ON...

1. **Conclusions** What did Walter do that showed he was considerate and understanding?

2. **Comparisons** How were Walter and Cloyd alike? How were they different?

LOOK AHEAD Read to page 43 to find out why Cloyd wants to start to work at the farm.

Cloyd is ready to work, but Walter has another idea.
He lets Cloyd choose one of his horses.

5

Walter knocked early on Cloyd's door. Cloyd woke to a warm house cheerful with the smell of sausage and eggs. Walter had **fired up** the cookstove and cooked breakfast on it. Cloyd ate with an eye on the fire showing through the draft slot. The old man opened the warmer door by the stovepipe and brought out sweet rolls.

"My grandmother keeps the frybread warm in there," Cloyd said.

"She **raised** you, didn't she?"

Cloyd nodded. He was beginning to feel uncomfortable. It sounded like Walter knew about his mother, how **she died getting him born**, how his father had run off. Walter wouldn't know what had happened to his father. He was the only one who knew that, and

---

fired up started a fire on
raised took care of
she died getting him born she died when he was born

he wasn't going to tell anybody, not even his sister or grandmother.

"Where does your sister live?" Walter asked gently.

"Salt Lake. She goes to a boarding school. I haven't seen her for a long time."

"That's too bad."

Cloyd felt more uncomfortable. He didn't want any pity. He wanted to talk about something else. "What are my jobs?" he asked.

The old man **stroked the white stubble** on his chin. "What needs doing worst around here is the foundation wall down in the basement. It has a bad crack in it. I don't know about you, but summer's no time to work indoors to my way of thinking, so I'm **gonna put that one off**. **Irrigating** the hayfields will keep me plenty busy, so I want to find you a project you can work on your own at. I've got something in mind, but I need to **chew on** it a little longer. Let's take a look around while I think about it—I'm just **getting the hang of** things myself after lettin' the farm set last year."

They went outside. Cloyd followed Walter up the

....

stroked the white stubble touched the hair
gonna put that one off going to wait to do that job
Irrigating Watering
chew on think about
getting the hang of becoming used to

stairway inside the big red barn. The loft upstairs was huge, and empty except for a dozen or so bales of hay off in one corner. Swallows were flying in and out by the hundreds. There were nests everywhere with baby birds.

"Sure feels empty, don't it?" Walter remarked. "I used to fill all this up with hay—fed a lot of cows. You see, Cloyd, I didn't **hardly hit a lick** last summer."

"How come?"

"**On account of losing my wife. Hit me awful hard.** Thought I didn't have anything to live for, to tell you the truth."

Cloyd didn't know what to say. He pointed with his lips to the meager haystack. "You don't have enough for your horses . . . for the winter."

"Oh, you saw the horses then. Yes, sir, it's time I baled some hay. Pretty soon the fields'll **run to foxtails** if I don't, and then they won't be worth **a darn** to anybody."

"Did you ever have any kids?"

---

hardly hit a lick do much

On account of losing my wife. Hit me awful hard. I was very sad because my wife died.

run to foxtails get weeds

a darn anything

"No, never did," he said softly. "**We'd of liked to**, but it just never happened." There was a long silence, and Cloyd regretted the question.

"Say, I've got something I want to show you," Walter announced, and led Cloyd downstairs to the **tack room**.

Everywhere Cloyd looked were saddles and bridles and gear he didn't even know what to call. It was a wealth of leather, and he liked the smell of it. "I always used to ride bareback. . . ." he said cautiously. "I don't know anything about this stuff."

Walter **beamed**. "I could sure show you. If you'd like to ride, you could **take your pick of** the horses. Most are packhorses, but there's a few good saddle horses among 'em, and they need riding—I can't seem to find the time."

"What are packhorses?"

"Why, they're for carryin' loads—into the mountains, where there's no roads."

The mountains, Cloyd thought. He's all set up for the mountains. He's got the gear and the horses, and maybe he would take me. . . . "Do you go to the mountains?"

"That's a long story. . . . I've been keepin' horses for years, thinkin' I was going to get back up there and reopen

....

We'd of liked to We wanted to have children
tack room room with equipment for the horses
beamed smiled
take your pick of choose one of

a mine I've got up in the high country."

"You like mining?"

A big smile lit the old man's face. "You bet I do."

"What do you like about it?"

"Why, the gold, I suppose. Sounds crazy, but the price of gold yesterday was four hundred fifty-six dollars an *ounce*. When I was minin', gold was around thirty-two dollars. Makes a difference, don't it?"

"How come you quit if you liked it?"

"I got married, Cloyd. My wife made me promise to **give it up**."

The old man lowered his voice. "**She was scared to death of mines, thinkin' they're cavin' in all the time.** But what she never understood was that the Pride of the West won't cave in—never. I used to tell her it was safer than this house. There's not a stick of **timberwork** in that whole mine—it's a hard-rock gold mine if ever there was one. But now, back to the horses . . . how'd you like to look 'em over? We could take a feed bag and a halter up to the pasture and you could pick one out. I'm going to do some irrigating later, but you could—"

....

give it up stop mining

She was scared to death of mines, thinkin' they're cavin' in all the time. She worried that the mine would fall in.

timberwork wood

Cloyd shook his head. "What about my job?"

"We could **line that out** tomorrow. I want to see what you think of these horses."

They each had a feed bag and a halter. They found the horses in the shade of the big pines along the river upstream. There were ten of them. "They'll be pretty **skittish**," Walter said. "Haven't been rode."

Cloyd knew immediately which one he wanted: the blue roan, a big, well-muscled **gelding**. White hairs intermingled with gray underneath gave the roan a blue **tinge** all over. He wanted to call the horse to him, but he felt embarrassed having the old man see him. What if the horse wouldn't come? He had to try. "Hey—a, hey—a," Cloyd called softly. "Hey—a, hey—a." While the others shied away, the big roan came to him, slowly and alertly, its head held high to one side. Its nostrils flared as it caught the scent of the grain. Cloyd let the horse almost finish the grain before he slipped the halter over its head.

"Nice," Walter said. "Very nice. You made that look

....

line that out talk about your job
skittish nervous
gelding male horse
tinge color

easy. I'm partial to that sorrel mare yonder—got a real easy **gait**."

They led the two horses back to the barn. Cloyd admired the roan's lines, the way it **carried itself**. At every moment it seemed about to bolt, yet never did. The horse wasn't giving up its freedom, he thought. We chose each other.

First they **curried** the horses, then Walter showed him all about how to bridle and saddle his horse. The old man talked slow and made it easy to understand. "This blue roan's a smart'un. See how he puffs out his gut so you won't **cinch him tight**? And then the saddle falls off later and you with it."

Cloyd laughed. "Better not let him hear you. . . ."

"He thinks he's fooled us," Walter whispered. He turned away as if he was done, then winked and quickly cinched in a few more notches. "**I wasn't born yesterday**," he said.

Outside, Walter coached him on how to mount the big roan. "Confidence is the main thing. He's gonna be skittish—been too long since he had a man on his back.

....

gait way of walking
carried itself walked, moved
curried brushed
cinch him tight put the saddle on too tightly
I wasn't born yesterday The horse will not trick me

One quick move, and don't quit halfway. Let him feel your confidence."

As excited as he was, Cloyd calmed himself. He tried to talk to the big roan with his heart. You and me, blue horse, he thought. You're the most beautiful horse I've ever seen. I bet you can run fast. We'll be friends, you and me.

In one motion, much the way he used to when he rode bareback, he swung up into the saddle. The big roan lifted his head and took a step or two, then **settled right down.** Cloyd patted him on the neck.

"Well, I'll be," Walter chuckled. "He really **took a shine to** you. That horse never **gave me the time of day.**"

"Does he have a name?"

"**Never got around to it.** None of 'em do."

They rode up the river trail through the big pines alongside the rapids. They followed the river for many miles, until the trail left it and climbed more than a thousand feet. The horse was surefooted and enjoyed the work. Cloyd was thrilled with the feel of the horse. He liked riding with the old man. He liked the wind in the

....

settled right down was calm
took a shine to likes
gave me the time of day liked me; noticed me
Never got around to it. I never named him.

trees and the gray jays and the way he felt. He hadn't felt this good in a long time. Finally he caught a glimpse of the river again, all white, in a gorge so deep and narrow it stirred his heart to beating loud. Like thousands of knives, the dark walls were flinty and jagged, so unlike the smooth sandstones of home. Cloyd remembered the snowy peaks he'd seen towering over the mountains. This gorge, he realized, was only the beginning of that higher country. He took the blue stone from his pocket and turned it slowly in his hand. Someday, he **vowed**, he'd see those peaks up close. He would see the home of the Utes.

The sun was dropping fast. They had to turn around and head back for the farm. He did a lot of thinking on the way. He would work hard for the old man, harder than the old man could ever have dreamed, and then he would ask the old man to take him to the mountains.

"Blueboy," he whispered, naming the horse. "You and me, Blue. We'll get to the mountains. Blueboy and Lone Bear."

It was dusk. They were back down on river level, not far from the farm. Blueboy **reared**, and then Cloyd saw

....

vowed told himself; promised
reared stood up on his back legs

a black form ahead **lope** across the trail with an unusual gait, followed by another, smaller black shape. "A bear!" he said, his voice filled with amazement. "A bear with a cub, isn't it?"

"Black bear," Walter said. "Sure enough."

"I've never seen one before. There aren't any bears back home."

"**Somethin' else, ain't they?** They live here, sure enough, but you don't see 'em that often. Born for the wild."

....

lope run
Somethin' else, ain't they? Aren't they interesting?

BEFORE YOU MOVE ON...

1. **Inference** Reread pages 35 and 39. Why did Cloyd keep asking what his job would be?

2. **Character's Point of View** Why were horses and bears important to Cloyd?

LOOK AHEAD Read pages 44–52 to see how Cloyd starts working for Walter.

Cloyd starts building Walter's fence. He hopes that someday Walter will help him meet a special goal, too.

6

Cloyd woke feeling good all over. As he yawned and stretched himself awake, he remembered **his fleeting glimpse of** the bear and the cub. What an amazing sight they were, he thought, and how lucky he'd been to see them. Or was it luck? He took the bearstone from under the pillow and turned it in his fingers. Lone Bear, he thought, that's the name I gave myself. These things were too wonderful to be accidents. His grandmother would understand. He recalled the feel of the powerful roan under him, and he heard the music in the old man's chuckle. He felt good, he felt strong. Now he wanted to **prove himself**.

"What's that job you were going to tell me about?" Cloyd asked at breakfast.

....

his fleeting glimpse of when he saw
prove himself show the old man that he could work

"Well, I'll need your help **come haying time**, bucking bales and putting up the hay, but of course that won't be until July. But I do have a project you could make a start on for me—**I've been putting it off** for a couple years now. Need to build a fence. I'm so busy irrigating the field, haying, fixing tractors and whatnot, I can't seem to get around to it."

"Show me about the fence. I can do that."

After breakfast, Cloyd followed Walter to a shed, where Walter picked out a **posthole digger** and a long steel bar. Cloyd grabbed the bar. It was six feet long and heavy, and he thought he could carry it better than the old man could. They walked through the lower field to the peach orchard and Walter's property line beyond it.

Walter set the tools down on the riverbank and led Cloyd along his line of short wooden survey stakes, one for each posthole that had to be dug, all the way across the end of the field from the river to the distant ditchbank at the base of the mountain. Then they walked back to the starting point. "What's this fence for?" Cloyd asked.

Walter's face went red suddenly as he looked away. Cloyd watched him closely.

....

come haying time when it is time to bale the hay
I've been putting it off I have been waiting to do it
posthole digger tool to dig holes

"Well, Cloyd, I need to **fence off a fellow that's been takin' advantage of me**. This fellow—lives across the highway—he moves in from California a few years ago, buys himself a farm, and starts going broke, because he's no kind of farmer and won't listen if you try to help him, so he gets the idea he'll **set himself up as a big-game guide**—"

The old man ran short of breath, sputtered. Veins stood out on his forehead.

"He advertises in the big-city newspapers in Texas like he's **an outfitter,** which he ain't licensed for, then he drives his hunters across my place in their four-wheel drives, tearin' up the field so bad you can't hay for the ruts. I only drive on the field myself when it's bone-dry. Then they park their trucks and horsetrailers right by the headgate where the trail takes out. He tells them I live on a county road **with public access**! The sheriff and the game warden, they've warned this fellow, but come fall he'll try it again. The sheriff says what I really need is a fence to go with my gate, and I guess he's right."

....

fence off a fellow that's been takin' advantage of me stop someone from coming in

set himself up as a big-game guide help hunters find big animals like bears and deer

an outfitter someone who leads hunters

with public access that everyone can go on

Walter's color returned, his breathing came easier. "You see, Cloyd, I've got the only access to a big piece of country up the Piedra here. There's no gov'ment trailhead anywhere near. So to get up the river to public land, folks have always had to come through my place. I don't mind when they ask beforehand and park downriver and walk or ride through, but this fellow doesn't know the meaning of courtesy. **He's only out for himself.**"

Cloyd had watched with interest as Walter's anger rose. He could picture the neighbor from the other side of the highway driving up in the fall with his hunters and finding a new fence and a locked gate. The man would get out of his truck, walk along the fenceline, and see there was no way to get around it. Then he would have to turn around, and Walter would have won.

"Of course it's a two-year project, anyway," Walter said. "But we can make a start."

"I could finish this fence," Cloyd insisted.

"I don't think so. There's a lot of work in a fence like that. First off, since it's river bottom, you'll **run into** rocks

....

Walter's color returned Walter calmed down
He's only out for himself. He only cares about himself.
run into find

sometimes, and to go deep enough to hold a post you'll have to break the rock with that bar and pull it out in pieces. Then there's all the posts to **log out of** the woods, wire to run—there's a lot of work in it. You'll be a help to me if you get some of the holes dug."

Walter dug the first hole to get Cloyd started. "No rocks in this'un," he said. **"Lucked out."**

Cloyd took the posthole digger from the old man, pulled out the next stake, and started to dig.

"Say," Walter said, "Whyn't you hold off until I can fetch a pair of gloves for you and a jug of ice water. And a cap, too. I always wear one when I'm standin' out in the sun irrigatin'."

"I never wear a hat."

"There probably won't be much cloud cover until later in the month . . . usually doesn't start raining until the Fourth of July."

Cloyd shook his head. "I don't like hats."

"Suit yourself," Walter answered cheerfully. "Well, I better let the water into the field, or the grass is gonna burn up."

....

log out of cut from trees in
"Lucked out." "We are lucky."
Suit yourself Do what you want to do

Cloyd let the old man disappear through the orchard, then started digging with all of his strength and determination. If he was going to get finished, he'd better get started. He could tell Walter had already forgotten he was going to bring back some gloves, but it didn't matter. He didn't like to use gloves.

The June days and Cloyd's line of completed postholes advanced steadily. His blisters healed, his hands grew **callused**. The white stubble on the old man's face lengthened into thick white whiskers. He said he was **having a lark**: he had never grown a beard in his whole life, and now he was going to. Cloyd liked the way it made him look. Like an old miner. He would look perfect, Cloyd thought, with a pick over his shoulder and leading a donkey.

Even though he didn't work with Walter during the day, Cloyd wasn't lonely. **His mind was brimful of thinking** as he worked the rhythm of the posthole digger. He thought about Blueboy and where they would ride

....

The June days and Cloyd's line of completed postholes advanced steadily. Throughout June, Cloyd made more holes.

callused hard

having a lark growing a beard for fun

His mind was brimful of thinking He kept thinking

that evening, and wondered if he would see another bear. The mountains he thought about, too, all the time. He'd made a promise to himself not to mention his plans to Walter until he had the fence finished, until he had proven himself, until he'd earned the mountains.

Every so often the blades of his posthole digger would strike a rock, and then Cloyd was in for a battle. First he'd try to dig another hole, but often he'd strike the same rock. Then there was no choice but to break it with the bar, and he would slam the bar down with all his **might**. He found a fierce satisfaction in breaking rock. And he knew **the sound carried up to Walter in the field**. The old man was surprised with how hard he could work and how many holes he had dug. Cloyd had never worked this hard before; he was surprising himself. In the early afternoon Walter would ring the porch bell, and they would eat a big meal. Then he'd go back to his postholes and work until Walter called him for supper.

In the evenings Cloyd would hurry out to saddle up the roan and take him for a ride. Blueboy could run **like anything**. The horse liked him, and he knew it. Cloyd felt

···

might strength

the sound carried up to Walter in the field Walter could hear him working from far away

like anything fast

good **streaming** along the river road with the wind in his hair. He talked to the horse all the time. The horse was the only one who knew his secret name and his secret plans.

Late in the evenings, Walter would read his mining journals. Cloyd liked to ask him what it was like in the high country. "Tell me about the mountains up real high," he'd say, "like where your mine is."

Walter would stroke his whiskers. "Oh, there's nothin' like it. Most beautiful country I've ever seen."

"Is there much water?"

"Oh, there's water everywhere. Little trickles runnin' off snowbanks, ponds, lakes, creeks, streams, baby rivers. . . . Some places the ground's so wet it's like walkin' on a sponge. It's as green as can be, and there's wildflowers everywhere you look."

"How high are the tops of the mountains?"

"Punch holes in the sky."

"Can you climb to the top?"

"If you got wings."

"What happens to the animals when winter comes?"

"Freeze solid," said the old man, **with his tongue in his cheek**. "Wouldn't you?"

....

streaming riding
"Punch holes in the sky." "Very high; they reach to the sky."
with his tongue in his cheek trying to make Cloyd laugh

It was a good time, talking about the mountains in the parlor. Walter would set his mining journal aside, the tiredness would leave his eyes, and **a faraway look would come over him** as he spoke. Cloyd liked to see him scratch his whiskers. He liked this old man, Walter Landis.

....

a faraway look would come over him he looked like he was dreaming

BEFORE YOU MOVE ON...

1. **Character's Motive** Why did Cloyd decide to work so hard on the fence?

2. **Cause and Effect** Reread pages 49–50. How did working on the fence affect Cloyd?

LOOK AHEAD Read pages 53–63 to find out what makes Cloyd angry.

Cloyd works hard to finish the fence.
When Cloyd gets a letter, Walter makes a
new discovery about Cloyd.

7

The days were scorching. Weeks passed with no cloud cover at all. Cloyd kept working. **The shade of the nearby timber beckoned, but he resisted.** He was getting closer all the time to digging that last posthole. In the evenings he'd sneak looks at the calendar; he kept trying to guess how long it would take him to build the fence. Day by day he was realizing it was a much bigger project than he'd thought at first, just as the old man had said.

Sundays were something to look forward to, the only **break in the routine**. Walter would go into Durango for groceries and supplies, and Cloyd would spend the day with Blueboy.

At breakfast, Walter was all dressed up for town and

....

The days were scorching. The days were very hot.

The shade of the nearby timber beckoned, but he resisted. Cloyd wanted to go to the shade, but he didn't.

break in the routine time when Cloyd could stop working

working on a shopping list. It was another Sunday, but Cloyd wasn't feeling very good about it. He woke up feeling bad, and he didn't know why. He only knew he wasn't very happy.

They hardly spoke over breakfast. **The talk between them was dying out little by little.** There was only the work.

He knew Walter could tell he was feeling bad. The old man was a long time buttering his toast. At last he said, trying to sound cheerful, "Gonna take Blueboy out today, Cloyd?"

Cloyd shrugged.

"I sure hope so. Say, I've been wondering if you might like to **give that fenceline a rest**. Maybe do a little of this and a little of that, take some more time with the horse."

"I don't want to," Cloyd said stubbornly.

Walter left for Durango. Cloyd knew he didn't want to ride Blueboy. He didn't feel good enough. There was a little flame of anger in him that was starting to grow. The old man was saying he should give up. Walter didn't really expect anything from him. Walter had heard all about school, how he'd failed everything. Now Walter expected

---

The talk between them was dying out little by little. They did not talk very much.

give that fenceline a rest stop working on the fence

him to fail here, too. Well, they were all wrong about him, wrong to say he was lazy. He wanted to **show the old man**.

Cloyd shouldered the posthole digger and dragged the bar along behind. He didn't have that many holes to go. He wanted to get the posts in the ground before Walter needed his help with the hay. Then that would leave only stringing the wire.

Concentrating on his welding, Walter was startled to notice Cloyd standing beside him. Removing his mask, Walter switched off the arc welder. "How's it going, Cloyd?" he asked cheerfully.

"I finished those holes."

Walter beamed. "Well, Cloyd, that's downright amazin', is what it is. **I never seen the like.**"

"We should finish the fence. So you'll have it before hunting season."

"I'd sure like to see it finished, too, Cloyd, but there's a lot of work left in it, **fallin' junipers for posts and whatnot**."

"I can start cutting the posts tomorrow."

The old man cast his eyes to the ground, removed his

....

show the old man show Walter what he could do

I never seen the like. I have never seen someone work like that.

fallin' junipers for posts and whatnot cutting down juniper trees to use them as fence posts and other things

cap, ran his hand slowly over the top of his head and back. "Cloyd," he said finally, "I wish you'd let me cut the posts. After we get the hay in and it gets to rainin', I won't have to irrigate so much. I'll take out some junipers on the hill, clean 'em up so you can set 'em, then we'll string the wire together."

"You don't think I can do this job?"

"It's the chain saw I'm worried about. They're dangerous, Cloyd. I've used one for years, and I'm still scared of it. You see, sometimes a tree has a mind of its own, and there's plenty of ways you can make a mistake. Have you ever handled one?"

"You can show me," Cloyd insisted.

Walter saw how much it meant. At last he had to say, "Cloyd, I believe you can do just about anything you **set your mind to**."

Cloyd felt good as he walked up the field through the glowing late light to the barn. He took the bearstone out and turned it in his fingers, held it against his cheek. There was just enough evening left for him to visit the roan. "Hey-a, hey-a," he called, and the horse nickered back.

The roan was waiting by the pasture gate. Cloyd fed him a little grain and then curried him, thinking aloud

....

set your mind to decide to do

all the while. "You and me, Blue, we're gonna go to the mountains. I'm gonna finish it, finish everything; then we can go to the mountains, you and me."

In the morning Walter poked around the machine shed and collected the saw, an axe, a plastic bottle of bar-and-chain oil, a pint can of engine oil, an empty gas can, and a leather bag of tools. He told Cloyd all about the saw, and it seemed to Cloyd to take forever. Two or three times Walter cautioned Cloyd to mix the engine oil in with gas. "**Straight gas'll ruin her,**" he said. Cloyd didn't ask questions, and Walter didn't ask if he understood.

Walter knew the Utes **weren't big talkers**. He'd lived his whole life near the Colorado Utes, and **his occasional contacts with them had taught him how to take things**. The way Cloyd pointed with his lips—only the old Utes did that anymore, something about it being rude to point with the hand or finger. And like the old-time Utes, Cloyd looked away when he talked or was spoken to.

Yet for all the time they'd spent together, Walter wished he understood Cloyd better. In the evenings Cloyd

....

Straight gas'll ruin her If you don't mix the oil and gas, the saw will break

weren't big talkers did not talk very much

his occasional contacts with them had taught him how to take things they had taught him how many of the Utes acted

no longer asked about the mountains; he was **bone-weary** from working too hard. The boy would fall asleep watching the television. He himself was tiring, too, even **questioning the need to set the farm back to rights**. He was back to the old routines again, standing in the hot sun all day long and tediously moving dirt and routing water. And Cloyd was working relentlessly, harder every day, for reasons of his own. **To whatever end, their course was set.** Cloyd couldn't be turned now. The only time he'd take for himself was a short visit mornings and evenings with the big roan. He'd work the currycomb and talk, talk, talk with the horse. If I could interview that horse, Walter mused, I'd know the boy a whole lot better.

Cloyd thought it would take only a few days to log out the posts he needed. He soon found out it wasn't going to be that easy. The junipers grew only here and there on the mountain. He wished he could use the jack pines or the straight young firs. But he knew why the old man wanted junipers—they'd never rot.

....

bone-weary very tired

questioning the need to set the farm back to rights
wondering if he needed to work on the farm

To whatever end, their course was set. They would both
continue to work on the farm, no matter what happened.

He had to **range** the hillside the length of the farm, hundreds of feet up the slope, to find his trees. If anything, the work was harder than digging the postholes. The saw was heavy and noisy; his ears were always ringing. He burned his thumb on the exhaust and cut the heel of his hand sharpening the chain. After he **felled** a juniper, he had to top it to a seven-foot length, trim it, then drag it down the hillside to the ditch. The heavy posts often snagged in the oakbrush and brought him tumbling down. Even though he had only fifty-seven posts cut, he knew he had to get off the hillside for a while. He decided to **set the posts he had**.

Placing a rock at the bottom of each hole the way the old man had suggested, Cloyd set the posts. He kept his eye on the tractor up the field as the old man drove around cutting the hay. Walter would need his help in a few days to buck the bales onto the trailer and stack them in the barn.

Cloyd set the fifty-seventh post as the sun was setting on the next-to-last day of June. The posts reached less than halfway to the ditchbank. He wanted to go back up

---

range look all over

felled cut

set the posts he had put the posts he had in the ground the hillside the next day and cut more posts, until he had all he needed, but he knew he'd lost. He could go back to the fenceline after haying, but it wouldn't be the same. He had wanted to **get through with it before haying, and he'd lost**. Now there would be too much work on the fence after haying. The work would be hot and endless, and there wouldn't be time left for him and Blueboy to go to the mountains. He'd been **fooling himself** about the mountains all along. The old man would never have let him go anyway.

The sun was down, the air was cooling fast. Exhausted, Cloyd leaned on the last post. He felt chilled one minute, burning up the next. He feared he might have fever from the **ticks** in the oakbrush. When he looked down the line of fenceposts, it seemed senseless, what he'd done. The day before, he'd received a letter from his sister, and he didn't even know what it said. He could read a few words, but that was all. He was too embarrassed to ask the old man to read it to him. He **longed for** White Mesa. All he wanted was to go home. Looking across the field to the gray farmhouse in the trees, he wondered what had made

....

get through with it before haying, and he'd lost finish the fence before he worked on the hay, but he could not

fooling himself foolishly dreaming

ticks insects

longed for missed

him think he could **belong** here.

Walter was in the house, fixing a special supper for Cloyd. He'd been planning it all week: a Thanksgiving-style dinner with turkey and all the extras. He'd taken the day off to prepare the meal, but he hadn't been able to talk Cloyd out of working on the fenceline. When Cloyd finally came in, later than usual, he **hadn't even a nod for** the old man. Walter could see how gloomy he was. Cloyd shoved his plate away after picking at the turkey. Walter, who never ate much, began to put away the mountain of leftovers.

In the parlor, Walter **sought out his recliner**. Cloyd collapsed with a sigh on the sofa. Walter glanced at his new *Mining Gazette* but set it aside. Something was terribly wrong, and he'd have to get the boy to tell him what it was. What could he say? Maybe he should try a new tack. "Tell me about that letter you got yesterday," he suggested awkwardly. "What do you hear from home?"

Cloyd battled the confusion washing over him. He felt angry at the old man, and he didn't know why. He thought about the letter in his pocket. What should he say?

....

belong feel like he was at home
hadn't even a nod for did not even talk to
sought out his recliner sat in his chair

"It's my letter," he said finally. "It's none of your business."

Walter felt sorry he had chosen the letter to try to talk about. "I didn't mean to **pry**, Cloyd," he apologized.

"I don't know what's in the letter!" Cloyd shouted, standing up. "I can't read it. I don't know how. There, are you satisfied?"

He felt the weight of the old man's eyes on him.

Leaning forward, the old man reached out and touched Cloyd's hand. The dark veins stood out on his forehead. "I'm sorry, Cloyd," he whispered. "**I had no idea.** Let me read it for you. Where's the letter?"

Cloyd wanted to hear the letter, but he **hated his weakness being suddenly out in the open**. Now the old man would think that he was stupid.

"Why, I could maybe help you in the evenings," Walter was saying. "And I could sure read you these mining papers. . . ."

"I don't want your help," Cloyd said. He had to get away.

---

pry ask about something private

I had no idea. I did not know that you couldn't read.

hated his weakness being suddenly out in the open did not like that someone knew that he could not read

In his confusion he bumped into the table and spilled the old man's coffee all over the mining newspapers. He had to get to his room and be **by himself**.

"Leave me alone," he shouted at Walter as he ran for the stairs. "Leave me alone!"

....

by himself alone

BEFORE YOU MOVE ON...

1. **Conclusions** Reread pages 54–55. Cloyd got angry when Walter wanted him to rest. Why?

2. **Plot** When did Walter notice a change in Cloyd? What did Walter do about it?

LOOK AHEAD What happens when hunters come to the farm? Read pages 64–71 to find out.

Cloyd is surprised to see bear hunters at the farm.
Cloyd thinks that he does not know Walter at all.

8

In the morning Cloyd was surprised to find Walter acting
as if nothing had happened. "Time to buck them bales
out of the field and up into the barn," the old man said
cheerfully. Cloyd didn't respond. How could **things ever
be the same between them again**? He **kept his eyes on his
plate** and said nothing.

After breakfast, three pickups pulling horsetrailers
drove into the farm. Two of the trucks were loaded heavily
with saddles and camping equipment. The third carried
at least a dozen barking hound dogs. Six men in blaze-
orange vests got out of the trucks as the old man waved
and walked down the drive to meet them. Had the old
man **been expecting them**? Cloyd wondered. He hadn't
talked about anyone coming.

---

things ever be the same between them again they act the
same way they did before

kept his eyes on his plate looked down

been expecting them known that they were coming

The leader, very tall and sure of himself, stood in front of the rest and **made small talk** with the old man. Cloyd watched from behind a tractor in the shop. The tall man took off his cowboy hat, revealing a headful of wavy red hair. The wind, blowing in Cloyd's direction, carried their words to him. The two talked easily about Walter's new beard and his peaches. Apparently they were good friends.

The others standing around began to **fidget**, Cloyd saw. They were strangers. One of them asked in a Texas accent, "Does the wind always blow like this in Colorado?"

Cloyd saw the tall, red-haired man turn his shoulder and wink to Walter. "A question like that you oughta ask Walter here. Heck, I was just a kid when he invented this whole country. What about this wind, Walter—think it'll **let up**?"

The old man tugged at his cap. "It's been known to blow, that's for certain. Just workin' up to it this morning. Myself, I like to **keep track of the wind** by hangin' a chain on a post. If it stands out straight, that's a breeze, but when it gets to whippin' around and links snap off, why

....

made small talk talked about things that were not important
fidget get bored
let up stop
keep track of the wind see how windy it is

look out—it's likely to get windy by sundown."

Walter told it straight-faced, but when he finished he held his breath, and his ears turned red. Everyone was laughing. The old man's cheeks were all puffed out. Finally he blew the air out his nose, his head bobbing, and he stroked the white whiskers on his chin. "Yes sir," he concluded, "It can blow—not that it does very often."

Cloyd was amazed at how easily the old man **got on with** these people, laughing with them and having a good time. He hadn't even met some of them before. Who were these people?

Still laughing, the men **turned to their preparations**. Cloyd came out of the shed and watched them unload the horses. After they parked their trucks and trailers out of the way, they packed the horses, shouting instructions back and forth. Walter came over to Cloyd and said the tall man was his old friend. Walter was all excited, like the man was really important. "Rusty's the best outfitter in the San Juans," he said. "Best outdoorsman I ever saw. **More'n likely he'll scare up a bear.**"

....

got on with talked to
turned to their preparations started to get ready
More'n likely he'll scare up a bear. He can easily find a bear.

The red-haired man beckoned to Walter from beside the coal pile, where he was **rigging the horses**. The old man went to him and then into the house, returning with the salt and pepper shakers from the kitchen table. Suddenly Cloyd realized that these men had to have the old man's permission to hunt on his land, and that he had already given it to them. To hunt for bears?

With no warning, the old man was bringing the red-haired man over. "Got someone I'd like you to meet, Rusty," he said to his friend. "This here's Cloyd."

For an instant, before he looked away, Cloyd saw the bear hunter's eyes. The man thought that meeting Cloyd was a joke. The tall man stuck out his giant hand, and said in his **raspy** voice, "Glad to meet 'ya. 'Cloyd,' is it? Never heard a name like that before."

Walter had never tried to shake hands with Cloyd. Cloyd hated shaking hands. But he had no choice but to **offer his** now.

The red-haired man didn't just shake his hand, he crushed it. He didn't have to do that, Cloyd thought. It hurt really bad. Cloyd tried not to let his face show the

....

rigging the horses getting the horses ready to go
raspy scratchy
offer his shake hands

67

pain. He glimpsed the man's mocking eyes. The eyes said Cloyd was nothing, nothing at all, only an Indian.

The old man was trying to get them to talk. "Cloyd here's real good with horses," Walter said, beaming. "That blue roan of mine has really taken a shine to him."

"Is that so?" the outfitter said with a short laugh. "Well, a horse ain't a dog, Cloyd. It **could care less** about you. All it cares about is getting fed. A horse is a work animal, not a pet."

Cloyd turned away. His hand was still throbbing. The bear hunter **turned to his own business** and mounted his horse. Cloyd imagined what he could do to the red-haired man's hand if he were twice the man's size. Break every bone in it.

Cloyd watched the riders and their dogs disappear upriver. He was furious, and the old man didn't even know it. Cloyd was sure now that **he meant nothing to the old man**. These men were his real friends. And they were bear hunters.

It was time to bring in the hay. The old man was going to drive the tractor, and he was supposed to buck the bales

....

could care less does not care

turned to his own business looked away from Cloyd

he meant nothing to the old man Walter did not care about him

onto the trailer and afterward stack them up in the barn. The old man, he recalled, liked to **brag** about how heavy his bales were—eighty pounds. "People get their money's worth," he'd said. Eighty pounds was fine for Walter—the old man wasn't planning on bucking the bales himself. That would be Cloyd's job.

The old man was standing by the tractor, waiting, but Cloyd walked off down to the riverbank instead. A few minutes later he heard the tractor's motor fire. The old man was going to **go ahead** without him. Let him try, Cloyd thought. It's his hay, not mine.

Along the riverbank he saw several **magpies and then a raven**. They reminded him of the canyons back home, and his sister, and he grew powerfully homesick. He brought the bearstone out of his pocket and tried to make a wish on it that he could go home. But the stone only reminded him of where he was and what the red-haired man was going to do. In a sudden burst of awareness he felt like he was the bear the man was after, and he could feel what it would be like to be chased by barking dogs and men on horses. He knew with awful certainty that

....

brag talk proudly

go ahead start working

magpies and then a raven different birds

the bear would be run down, cornered, and killed. Maybe it would be the mother bear, the one he'd seen with the cub. It was the old man's fault, he decided bitterly—he'd given his permission. If they killed a bear, the old man would **have to pay**. The old man never cared about me, he thought, these are his real friends.

Walter decided to bring in the hay all by himself. Something was wrong with Cloyd, he knew, but he shouldn't have walked off on him when he was needed most. Well, he would show this boy **what Walter Landis was made of**. He'd bucked a few bales in his life. Jumping off and back on the tractor, he pitched bale after bale onto the trailer like he was a young man again. His face was flushed bright red, his breathing came louder and louder, but he wouldn't quit. He brought load after load to the barn, heaving and grunting and dragging the bales into place. He'd work until all the hay was in or his heart burst, whichever came first. He didn't care which.

He worked all morning and never came in for a meal. He worked all through the long afternoon, through the dusk, and into the darkness, until the last bale was up in the barn. Then he walked silently into the house,

....

have to pay be sorry
what Walter Landis was made of that he could work, too

neglecting to take off his boots or his cap. Tracking dirt on the white parlor rug, he disappeared into his room, trailing bits of hay.

Walter was exhausted. He lay on his bed in his soiled overalls and boots and talked to his wife. "Maude," he said, "I'm an old fool, but I just don't know what to do with this boy. I sure wish you were here to help me. **Something's got into him**—I don't know what. He was doing so good. I guess we'll just hang on and see what happens. . . ."

The house fell silent. Cloyd was in his room, packing his duffel bag. The old man would **get rid of him** now. Tomorrow, he'd be back at Eaglewing. That would be all right. He didn't care anymore.

....

Something's got into him Something is wrong with him

get rid of him make him leave; send him away

BEFORE YOU MOVE ON...

1. **Conflict** Reread pages 69–70. Why was Cloyd furious with the hunters?

2. **Cause and Effect** What did Cloyd do after Rusty left? What effect did this have on Walter?

LOOK AHEAD Cloyd expects to be sent away. Read pages 72–76 to see what happens in the morning.

Cloyd and Walter go back to work. But when the hunters return, Cloyd thinks of a horrible way to punish Walter.

9

At **first light**, Walter was usually up and cooking sausage and eggs. Cloyd waited awhile for him in the kitchen, then took a loaf of bread and a jar of peanut butter outside. It was easy to put off seeing the old man.

Several hours later Walter limped out of the house. Cloyd was surprised to see he had shaved his beard off. "Hay's in the barn, Cloyd," he announced cheerfully. "Lucky it didn't get rained on. Once you're into July—and today's the first—**you're pressin' your luck**."

Cloyd didn't know what to say. The old man was acting like nothing had happened.

"**Wouldn't mind a bit** if it rained anytime now," Walter continued. "Wouldn't have to irrigate so much. I'd better start the water back in today—the field's drying

....

At first light Early in the morning; At dawn

you're pressin' your luck you take the risk that something bad will happen

Wouldn't mind a bit It would be fine

out bad. How 'bout you? **Got anything in mind?** Maybe you'd like to take that roan—"

"Make some more posts, I guess," Cloyd mumbled.

Walter hesitated. "Fine," he said uncertainly. "That's just fine."

Cloyd trudged across the field with the saw and the gas can. **He'd left behind** the pint of oil Walter wanted mixed with the gas.

It was another cloudless day. The last of the night's lingering cool air was burning off as he angled through the haystubble toward the hillside.

Before he climbed, he took a good look at his fenceposts, marching stout and straight all the way to the peach orchard. It was a strange feeling; they looked different. They didn't make him feel proud or good. They weren't his anymore.

He'd forgotten to bring along any drinking water. Already he was thirsty, and the sun was blazing. His head was pounding. Why was he still here? **He'd expected to be sent on his way** back to Durango, and instead he was being sent back to work as if nothing had happened.

....

Got anything in mind? Are you thinking about doing anything today?

He'd left behind He forgot to take

He'd expected to be sent on his way He thought that Walter would make him go

73

He had to get out of the sun. He **veered** away from
the hillside and followed the posts down to the orchard.
He dropped the saw, lay in the grass at the base of the big
boulder, and looked up at the trees. He could lie there
all day, he thought. Ever since he'd come to the old man,
there'd never been time to look at the world this way that
he liked.

Suddenly the bear was back in his thoughts, and
he could see it all happening. Men riding hard to **keep
up with** their **yapping** dogs, the bear exhausted and
desperate with no place to hide. He hated the outfitter,
that red-haired man, with all his heart.

His thirst brought him back to the orchard. He
swallowed hard and bitterly. The whole orchard was
exploding with growth. The countless rock-hard peaches
grew larger by the day—he'd been checking on them since
the first day he came to the farm. He'd admired them,
but now he hated them. These **thriving** trees of Walter's
with their long, green leaves were so superior to his
grandmother's it made him sick. Hers **were pitiful**.

He spat, but nothing came out. He had a bitter taste in

....

veered moved
keep up with go as fast as
yapping barking
thriving growing
were pitiful did not grow well

his mouth, like poison. His grandmother's peaches were rare and beautiful only in the way he used to see them, not as they really were. But the old man's trees could have all the water they wanted, while his grandmother's, with their **misshapen** trunks and **stunted**, yellowed leaves, stood here and there against the sun and depended on the rain. Sometimes the rains didn't come at all and the peaches shriveled on the trees and there was no moisture to suck out of them.

All at once he heard dogs barking and men calling— the outfitter and his bear hunters had returned. Cloyd ran up the road toward the house, where the men had dismounted and were showing off **their kill** to Walter. Everyone talked at once, except for the red-haired man, who was acting like it was **all in a day's work**. A bear was heaped atop a nervous horse. It wasn't as big as Cloyd would have thought. It looked about like a big black dog. The old man was going to let his friend butcher it right there and hang it up in one of his sheds.

As if he were invisible, he walked among the **preoccupied** hunters with them taking no notice of him.

....

misshapen badly shaped
stunted small
their kill the bear they had killed
all in a day's work just a normal part of his job
preoccupied busy

He approached the bear and stared at it. The bear had nearly bitten its tongue in two. Its mouth was choked with clotted blood. A fly walked on one of its eyes.

Recounting the hunt, the men poked fun at each other. One man, the one who'd asked the old man about the wind, was especially happy—he was the one who shot it. "Bearskin for the den," he said proudly.

"Plenty of good sausage, too, and some for Walter here," the red-haired man said in his raspy voice. "What don't make sausage I'll feed to my dogs."

Suddenly Cloyd remembered all the sausage he'd eaten at the old man's table. It almost made him retch to think it might have been—probably was—*bear* meat he'd eaten all those mornings. He backed out of the clearing in front of the house, turned and ran back toward the peach orchard. **A terrible revenge was taking shape in his mind.**

....

Recounting Talking about

A terrible revenge was taking shape in his mind.
He thought of a terrible way to show that he was angry.

BEFORE YOU MOVE ON...

1. **Conclusions** Reread page 73. How did Cloyd expect Walter to act? What does this show about Cloyd?

2. **Character's Point of View** Why did Cloyd feel angry about Walter's peach trees?

LOOK AHEAD Walter wants revenge on Cloyd. Read to page 82 to see what he does.

Cloyd snatched up the saw from the tall grass at the base of the boulder. He filled it with gas, pink instead of its usual purple, the way it looked with the oil added in. Right now he didn't care how Walter wanted it. The old man was just fussy—he wouldn't even drive his truck without checking the oil first. Everything Walter did had to be in neat lines, like his **windrows** and his fences. Everything had to be so clean, like the white rug in his parlor and his tractors, and everything had to be in its place in the house, the sheds, and the barn.

He grabbed up the saw and yanked the pull-cord with the saw in midair, as Walter had advised him never to do. The engine fired immediately and he gunned it until it screamed.

Cloyd wondered why he'd liked Walter **in the first place**, this fussy old white man who had a thousand times more than he needed and still had to have someone else do his work for him so he could get more. Maybe he'd worked for the old man because of finding the bearstone the first day. It was easy enough to see now—there was no connection between the good-luck token and the old man. Cloyd remembered how Walter laughed with the red-haired man and the other bear hunters when they

....

windrows rows of hay
in the first place at all

77

first arrived. Laughs with Bear Hunters should be the old man's secret name, he thought bitterly.

He cut through the skin of the nearest tree and **winced as he withdrew** the saw. Beads of moisture were forming along the edges of the fresh wound. From one to the next he ran with the saw roaring at full throttle, and he cut each of the twenty-two peach trees most of the way through. Each time, as the **saw's teeth bit into the thin bark**, he hollered with hurt as if he felt the saw himself. He didn't want to cut them down, he wanted them to die slowly. Before they died, their leaves would yellow and the peaches shrivel, and they would look just like his grandmother's peaches.

Now he knew he was in big trouble, but that made it easier. He **was only getting started**. This time there wouldn't be any doubt he was going back to Eaglewing.

His mind racing and his throat so dry it seemed **jammed with a wad of wool**, Cloyd stumbled out of the orchard with the heavy saw. When his fifty-seven posts came into view all standing straight and lined up so perfectly, he pulled up for breath and caught himself

....

winced as he withdrew pulled back in pain as he took out
saw's teeth bit into the thin bark saw started to cut a tree
was only getting started had more things to do
jammed with a wad of wool to have a piece of cloth in it

admiring them. But what was the fence really for? To keep a man from crossing a field. It was a stupid reason to have worked so hard. At White Mesa he went with the goats wherever he wanted. None of the Utes put up fences or claimed a part of the **mesa** for their own. The animals went where there was feed, and there were no fences at all until some white men chained the trees out by their roots, dragged them into the **arroyos**, and fenced the northern end of the mesa for beans.

Cloyd tried his shoulder against the first post. It wouldn't budge. He had set them deep, wedging rocks around the posts and packing them with clay soil. They'd set up like concrete. Why should Walter be so concerned about some people hunting deer and elk on his ranch while he thought it was fine for others to hunt bears? He was a fool to have worked for the old man.

The juniper posts wouldn't rot in two hundred years, but he didn't want them there at all. The field looked better without them.

The saw didn't want to start. After dozens of attempts Cloyd made it **idle erratically**, but it cut out as soon as

....

mesa land
arroyos creeks
idle erratically stop and move strangely

he tried the throttle. Eventually it caught at full throttle, and he discovered it would **run if he didn't let up** even a little bit. He walked along the line, sawing down the posts and thinking about people he didn't like. One post for the reading teacher who tried to make him read aloud, one for the speech teacher who always tried to make him get up in front of the class, and one for the nervous principal who was always saying, "Well, I guess I'll just have to use the board on you." One for each of the bear hunters. Two, three, four, five, six, sixteen for Walter and his friend, the red-haired man.

Half the posts remained when the saw **began to kill** as soon as it bit into the wood. Then it wouldn't fire at all. Cloyd checked the gas, which hissed as he loosened the cap. Boiling hot, most of it escaped. Maybe the saw did need oil mixed in with the gas, but who cared?

The saw was too hot; it wasn't going to start. Probably he'd ruined it by leaving out the oil. He felt like he was going to faint. He had to get out of the sun. He threw the saw down and walked off, **waded** the irrigation ditch at the edge of the field. Even though the water **ran** cool

....

run if he didn't let up cut posts if he did not stop
began to kill kept stopping
waded walked through the water in
ran was

and clear, he didn't think to drink any. He started up the mountainside toward the sandstone outcrop where he'd found the blue stone.

On his way up, Cloyd saw the trucks and horse-trailers leave, and then he saw the old man walk down to the peach orchard. He turned and fled higher. When he reached the top of the cliffs and looked out, **he was not soothed**, as he had expected to be. The sight of the distant peaks did nothing to **lift him out of the despair drowning him inside**. Usually after he did something he knew was going to bring trouble, he felt better in a way— revenged. But with the old man it was different. He'd never felt this awful in his life; he'd never liked anybody this much, as much as he'd liked Walter. Suddenly he felt more alone than ever before, even more than in the first days in Durango after the tribe had sent him to Eaglewing.

This wasn't the same as getting into trouble with the teachers or the principal, or with his housemother. Those people were making him do things he didn't want to do. It was different with the old man. Once, he had really

....

he was not soothed he did not feel better
lift him out of the despair drowning him inside make him feel better

wanted to work for Walter, and it was good then. Now everything was spoiled. He had spoiled it.

His thirst grew so bad he couldn't swallow. But he was good at **enduring** pain. No one could ever take that away from him. Maybe he would run away. But first he would **stand up to the old man for punishment** the way he did with the principal, then go home and hide in the canyons. Walter would take him back to Eaglewing, but he wouldn't stay for long. No one could find him in the canyons.

....

enduring living with

stand up to the old man for punishment take the punishment Walter would give him

BEFORE YOU MOVE ON...

1. **Flashback** Reread pages 78–80. What did Cloyd think about when he destroyed the trees and the fence?

2. **Conflict** What problem did Cloyd have after taking revenge?

LOOK AHEAD Read pages 83–94 to see if Walter punishes Cloyd.

Angry and sad, Walter takes Cloyd home to his grandmother. But Cloyd does not know if he wants to stay at White Mesa now.

10

It was dark, and Cloyd was off the mountain. As he reached for the latch on the front door, the old man stepped out of the shadows, trembling with rage. He caught the boy by the shoulders with unnatural strength and shook him back and forth against the door. "What the hell's the matter with you, anyway?" he roared.

Cloyd said nothing and let himself be shaken. **He'd spent his own anger and had none left to counter the enormity of the old man's wrath.**

Walter put his **livid** face against Cloyd's where the boy's eyes couldn't avoid his. "Who the hell are you to come in here and ruin our peaches? You knew damn well what those trees meant to me. Well? Speak to me!"

....

He'd spent his own anger and had none left to counter the enormity of the old man's wrath. He was not angry anymore and he could not yell back at Walter.

livid angry

Cloyd turned his head aside and looked at the ground.

"Give me that little blue rock you keep in your pocket," Walter commanded.

Cloyd's mouth turned sharply down at the corners. "What rock?" he grunted.

Walter extended his hand, palm up. "Give it to me, Cloyd. I wasn't born yesterday. I've seen you more'n once sneakin' it in and out of your hand. C'mon, give it!"

There was nothing else to be done. He could see **he owed it to the old man**. He heaved a sigh and fetched it out of his pocket.

Walter took the stone and closed his fist on it. "You care about this little rock, eh? You won't say? I think you do. C'mon, I want to teach you something."

Walter stalked over to his machine shop with the boy in tow, flicked on the bare bulb suspended from the rafters, and set the blue stone on his anvil. Then he reached for the sledgehammer.

"A dose of your own medicine," the old man raged, holding the sledgehammer high over his head.

Cloyd's heart turned to lead. He waited passively for his punishment.

....

he owed it to the old man   that Walter should have it

A dose of your own medicine   You will feel what I felt when you destroyed the peach trees

Cloyd's heart turned to lead.   Cloyd felt terrible.

As Walter focused on his target, he paused with the hammer in midair and craned his neck in the bad light. "What the hell is that thing?" he demanded.

"A bear," the boy answered quietly.

"A bear?" The old man took it in his hand and examined it up close. Cloyd edged forward.

"You care about this thing quite a bit, don't you?"

Cloyd wouldn't say. He backed off and looked at the ground.

"Oh, to hell with it," Walter **stormed**. "Here, keep it."

When Cloyd didn't respond, Walter reached over and shoved it into his pocket. "Go get your stuff. I just want to get the hell rid of you."

It was late at night. As the pickup **wound** slowly through the foothills on its way to Durango, each of them kept silent, **preoccupied with his own regrets**. Just after they passed through the little town of Bayfield, the headlights illuminated a rabbit darting across the highway. Walter and Cloyd both winced at the thump under the wheels. In their **broodings**, that thump

....

stormed yelled

wound drove

preoccupied with his own regrets thinking about what they had done wrong

broodings thoughts

resounded like a judgment, and each was plunged deeper **in remorse**.

Fifteen more slow and silent miles, and they reached Durango. Walter stopped at a red light and stared down Main at the blinking **yellows**. At this hour Durango was a ghost town, and it seemed there were only the two of them in the world. "I couldn't miss him," Walter said with a sigh.

"Miss who?" Cloyd asked quickly. Somehow he was eager to talk with the old man.

"Oh, that darned rabbit back there. He seemed bound and determined."

"It wasn't your fault."

"I suppose not," Walter said slowly. "**Just one of them things.** Well, show me the way to your . . . Eaglewing."

Cloyd gave directions, and then the old man geared the truck down, and it crept toward the group home. They both knew they had only a few minutes left. "I wonder if you'd mind if I looked over that turquoise piece of yours once more," Walter said.

The old man turned it over in his fingers, eyed it, and

....

in remorse into feeling sorry

yellows yellow traffic lights

Just one of them things. There are some things that you cannot stop.

rubbed it thoughtfully, but he said nothing as he drove down the empty streets.

"Turn here," Cloyd said.

Walter sighed. "It's a sure-enough bear," he said. "Could even be a grizzly, from the shape of it. I went to the Bear Dance once down at the reservation. . . ." he began, then stopped talking. **A revelation was forging itself in his mind.** At last he said, "You cut those peaches right after those fellows came in from their bear hunt. Isn't that right?"

Cloyd grimaced.

Walter scratched and scratched behind his ear, and then he handed the stone back. "Well, that **helps some**, it sure does."

"Here it is," Cloyd said, and pointed to the house with his lips.

Walter slowed to a stop and eyed the group home. It wasn't what he expected; you couldn't tell it apart from all the other tract homes in the neighborhood. He drove on another block before he stopped. For a long time he said nothing. He took off his cap and **raked** his bald head with

....

A revelation was forging itself in his mind. He started to understand why Cloyd cut down the trees.

helps some makes me understand a little bit better

raked scratched

his fingers. Then he said, shaking his head a little, "Pigs might fly, but they're unlikely birds."

"What's that mean?"

"Just an old saying," he replied with a faint smile. "I never did know exactly, but I always liked the sound of it. Cloyd, Susan told me once **you'd rather more'n anything just go home**. Is that right?"

Cloyd shrugged guardedly.

"Well?"

"They won't let me."

"I suppose not," Walter agreed, as he slipped the truck into gear and drove off.

"What're you doing?" Cloyd mumbled.

"Takin' you home."

"How come?"

"You ain't gonna do any good here at this 'Eaglewing,' are you?"

"They won't let you."

"I don't see nobody," Walter said gruffly.

"They'll come and get me."

"I'll wait a week before I tell Susan. You'll have some time at home, whatever happens."

....

you'd rather more'n anything just go home you just want to go home

They left Durango behind and headed west up a steep **grade**. Cloyd barely thought about going home, he was so astonished and puzzled. He didn't know what to **make of** this old man. He'd liked him, and then he'd hated him, and now he didn't know what to think. Walter was taking him home. After a few more miles had passed and they were on their way down the western side of the mountains, he asked again, "How come you're doing this?"

"Maybe it'll help you **get the bee out of your bonnet**," the old man said coldly.

Cloyd didn't want to have to ask him what that meant. The old man was in a strange mood—better to keep quiet. He thought about the horse. He wished **there'd been a chance to see** Blueboy before he left.

The sun was rising over the high desert as they neared White Mesa. In the clear, thin air Cloyd took in the landmarks he'd grown up with. He almost wished he could share them with Walter, but they hadn't really **made a peace**. To the north, Blue Mountain, the sacred one, still

....

grade hill
make of think about
get the bee out of your bonnet stop feeling so angry
there'd been a chance to see he could have seen
made a peace agreed to be friends again

wearing a patch of snow. To the east, the massive form of the Sleeping Ute lying on his back with arms folded across his chest, not yet ready to awake and vanquish his enemies. To the south, the glowing white cliffs of the San Juan as it flowed through Bluff, and beyond them the bare redlands of the Navajos with the towers of Monument Valley beginning to appear in the early light. To the west, the wooded slope of Cedar Mesa falling from the Bear's Ears to the river, gouged by the bottomless red-walled canyons. In those **remote** canyons was where he would hide, he decided. There, in the slick-rock country, he could live wild and free.

As they drove south out of Blanding onto the windy mesa, Cloyd searched for something to say to thank the old man. **There was something welling up inside him** that he'd never felt before and that had to be expressed. Too soon he was pointing out the **nondescript government house** that was his grandmother's, the one with the summer ramada of cottonwood branches on one side and the scraggly peach trees on the other. And then

....

remote far away

There was something welling up inside him He started to feel something

nondescript government house plain house built by the government

he was standing by the truck with his duffel bag in his hand, and the old man was saying, "Good luck, Cloyd. **Let's don't say good-bye with no hard feelin's.** . . . "

Cloyd nodded, but it was all happening too fast, his feelings were too deep to be reached. He found no words at all, only waved slightly as the old man turned the truck around and drove away.

The pickup was small in the distance by the time he realized he'd lost something of priceless value. He waved **forlornly**, then furiously, as the truck vanished. With the suddenness of a cloudburst in the desert, tears ran down his face.

He stumbled around behind the house to the little shed and corral, to **check in on the goats**. They were all gone. There was no fresh dung there, either.

After smoke started to come from the chimney pipe, he went in. His grandmother looked up from the frybread dough she was kneading and **gave a sharp cry**.

A Ute woman in the old style, she was dark, earthy, and large, the mainstay of her diet being frybread. In her

---

Let's don't say good-bye with no hard feelin's. We should not say goodbye with bad feelings toward each other.

forlornly sadly

check in on the goats look at the goats

gave a sharp cry yelled with surprise

green velveteen blouse and **voluminous** red skirt, and in the way she knotted her long hair and wrapped it in bright yarn, she reflected the influence of the nearby Navajos. Not one to ask a **flurry** of questions, she made a joke about his ribs showing through his T-shirt and opened up a can of fruit cocktail. It was something for him to start on while she cooked the frybread in the oil she had boiling on the cookstove. She fed the people in her life, **lavished affection on them**, rarely asked anything, and never tried to control whether they came or went.

They squeezed honey on their frybread. Cloyd wanted to talk. He'd spoken no Ute in the last year, as the boys from the Colorado reservation no longer knew the language. Right away he found himself telling her about Walter, how they'd worked together, how there was a river flowing right through his farm.

"Good," she said. "I knew you would like it in Colorado."

He told her about the high mountains, how someday he'd like to go there and climb the highest peak he could find.

....

voluminous big
flurry lot
lavished affection on them loved them a lot

"**Wouldn't that be something**," she said, her eyes reflecting the vision. "This man you work for, he lives in a good way?"

"He's the best man I ever knew," Cloyd heard himself saying. "He's old—older than you. His wife died. He's all alone."

Suddenly he knew he **had no desire to** hide out in the canyons. But what was he to do?

They talked about his sister who was at the boarding school in Salt Lake City. She had visited, his grandmother said, and had reported that everything was fine.

"I'll go to Blanding on Saturday and get lots of groceries so we can put some fat on your ribs."

Though sometimes someone she knew **stopped and picked her up**, often enough she walked all the way. Cloyd saw how he could save her the ten miles into Blanding, ten miles back. He realized he'd made a decision. "Oh, I can't stay long," he said. "I have to leave tomorrow."

His grandmother's eyebrows rose. "Oh?"

"Walter needs me. We have a lot of work to do."

"Well, that's good. I'm glad you came to see me.

....

Wouldn't that be something That would be wonderful
had no desire to did not want to
stopped and picked her up drove her

How are you traveling?"

Cloyd gave the hitchhiking sign with his thumb.

"I have to go now," she said. "I have a job. There is a day-care center here now. I cook for them. I had to sell the goats when there was nobody to take care of them. Maybe someday we'll get them back." She paused at the door. "Live in a good way," she said **in parting**, as she always did.

Cloyd decided to leave right away. His grandmother would understand. But would the old man **take him back**?

....

in parting when she left

take him back let him live there again

BEFORE YOU MOVE ON...

1. **Character's Motive** Walter was ready to destroy Cloyd's bearstone. What made him stop?

2. **Inference** What did Walter mean when he said on page 87 "Well, that helps some, it sure does."

LOOK AHEAD Read to page 102 to find out what happens when Cloyd goes to Walter's.

*At the farm, Walter feels sorry that Cloyd left.
When Cloyd returns, Walter makes exciting plans
for both of them.*

11

When Walter got home from Utah, he went directly
to his bed and collapsed in his dirty overalls. He was
exhausted. Unshaven, no sleep, nothing to eat, at his age
driving to Utah and back: **he'd been letting himself go
to the dogs**. And he didn't care. Right now he should be
irrigating the field. The grass would burn up in the heat
before long if he didn't. But he didn't care. He let himself
sink into sleep like a heavy stone plunging into a well.

When he woke up he was hungry. **Intent on drowning
himself in sentiment**, he went downstairs to the basement
to fetch a jar of peaches. He sat on a crate a long time
as the sunken window admitted less and less light. He
brooded on the two dozen or so jars of peaches left

....

he'd been letting himself go to the dogs he was not living in
a healthy way

Intent on drowning himself in sentiment Because he wanted
to feel sorry for himself

brooded on thought a lot about

on the shelf, her special Missouri peaches from those seedlings she'd brought along to Colorado. He'd told her that peaches wouldn't make it here, but she insisted. And there'd never been a time he'd gone downstairs for peaches that he hadn't remembered how it all happened.

Walter studied the crack that had appeared the length of the concrete basement wall just after his wife died. He got up and looked at it from across the room and then from the corner, where he **eyeballed** the length of the wall. He saw, or feared he saw, the foundation **bulging** in more than ever. As he had many times before, he outlined the work that had to be done to **plumb** the wall. Digging, pouring, timbering . . . He had the materials, the tools, the know-how—everything but the desire.

He didn't care anymore. About much of anything. He had for a while, when the boy was with him and they were working together to put the farm back in order. **To what purpose?** he wondered. He'd tried to make it like it was before, when his wife was alive, when the two of them and the farm were all one. On the surface, he and Cloyd had succeeded. But a farm isn't land and fenceposts and hay in

....

eyeballed guessed the measurements of
bulging pushing
plumb fix
To what purpose? Was it important?

the barn. As his wife always said, "A farm is a home." **He'd failed the boy.** When he'd had the chance to give him a home, he'd given him only work. **But work for work's sake can't keep a soul going**, Walter told himself. That's like pounding rocks in a prison yard. It's not the work that's awful, it's the lack of purpose.

She was gone. He could quit working the farm now. He himself had never been a farmer. He was a miner. He'd taken up farming for her, and gladly. They'd had all those good years making their living on the farm. Now he could quit, and lie down to rest. . . .

The next morning, Walter got up late and wandered outside to check on the horses. They had plenty of pasture and were able to drink from the river, but there was no telling when one might **turn** a leg in a varmint hole or get itself torn up in barbed wire. He felt bad when he saw the blue roan. He was never going to look at that horse again without thinking of the boy.

On the way back, he walked the irrigation ditch to see if a beaver hadn't moved in and started to dam it up. He sat down on the ditchbank with all the hayfields sloping

....

He'd failed the boy. He had not helped Cloyd.

But work for work's sake can't keep a soul going Working hard does not always help

turn break or sprain

away in front of him and tried to think of how to get his fields taken care of properly. **Only one choice remained, really**; he'd just been putting it off. He'd pick the best man he could and **lease the second cutting to him**. There were always industrious fellows around trying to raise more cows than they had the land to support. They had families to feed and mortgages to pay off. He'd turned down plenty of requests as they'd seen him getting older.

He didn't really have to work anymore. The farm had been paid for years ago, and he didn't need much income to live the way he did. They'd always put some savings by, and he got a steady, if small, income from the mining claim his wife had finally convinced him to sell, the one near Monarch Pass. She'd wanted him to sell the Pride of the West, too, but he was so adamant about keeping it, she finally gave up. She even quit **badgering** him about his packhorses and mining equipment, and his occasional announcements that in a year or two he might reopen his mine. So many years had gone by, she knew he was just hanging on to a dream he'd had when he was young, and there wasn't any harm to it.

....

Only one choice remained, really There was only one thing he could do

lease the second cutting to him let him rent the farm for the rest of the summer

badgering asking

It was pleasant to sit on the ditchbank in the morning sun and imagine he was up at the mine, sitting on the ore dump with Snowslide Creek rushing by and the peaks all around, the grass green and the wildflowers all in bloom. And inside the mine, not far at all from where he'd left off tunneling, waited the heart of the mountain, a secret place, a marvelous **fluke** made millions of years before in the **bowels** of the earth: a room having no doors, its furniture and draperies the fantastic shapes of glistening, crystalline gold.

Walter looked up to see a figure stumbling toward him out of the dying peach trees and through the sawed-off fenceposts lying at sixes and sevens down at the low end of the farm. The figure was struggling **with an awkward burden**. The old man squinted for a better look. In a few moments, to his everlasting amazement, he made out the white T-shirt and jeans, the duffel bag, the shaggy black hair and the brown face of the boy. He stood up meekly, lifted his cap, and ran his trembling hand over and over his skull. "He's come back, Maude," he said quietly. "He's come back." Then he walked down to meet the boy.

....

fluke strange thing
bowels deep parts
with an awkward burden to carry something

They stood face-to-face in the middle of the field.

"I want to try again," Cloyd said, looking away.

Walter shook his head **in wonder**.

"Please, I'll do better," the boy pleaded, thinking **he'd been turned down**.

"My goodness, Cloyd, of course you can. Maybe I can do better, too."

The boy pointed toward the orchard with his lips. "I'm sorry about the trees."

"I see you are. Both of us was hurt bad. I like to think, though, that the hurt you get over makes you stronger. Now let's get you taken care of. You look like something the cat spit out."

Cloyd smiled wearily, and they walked down to the house. He showered, ate some sandwiches, and went upstairs to bed. When he woke up, Walter had his clothes cleaned and dried for him. Cloyd asked what work he should do next. Walter explained that he was leasing out the farm and wouldn't be working it anymore. "I've been **thinking up a storm** today, Cloyd. I don't have that much time left in my life—I'm old enough, I oughta be able to do what I really want. Farmin' was good to me, but now

....

in wonder because he was surprised
he'd been turned down Walter would not let him stay
thinking up a storm thinking a lot

it's time to quit. **I ain't a mule turnin' grist.** What I'm tryin' to say is, do you remember how I've got a mine up in the back country?"

"The Pride of the West?"

"That's right. Remember how I said I'm gonna reopen it someday? I've been sayin' that for years. Well . . . *now*, I figure, now's the time. I'd need your help gettin' up there, of course, but if I remember right, you were always askin' about the mountains. I think it might **do us both a world of good** to get up into that high country. How would that suit you, Cloyd?"

"Will we take the horses?"

"Of course. No roads in there. We'll have to pack in everything."

Cloyd beamed. "Can I ride Blueboy?"

"**You bet.** I'll ride that sorrel mare."

"When can we go?"

"It might take a couple-three weeks to lease out the farm, get everything ready, and **tie up all the loose ends.** Tomorrow's the Fourth of July, so that still leaves us a good while up there before you have to be back in school.

....

I ain't a mule turnin' grist. I don't have to do the same thing all the time.

do us both a world of good be really good for us

You bet. Yes; sure.

tie up all the loose ends take care of the house and farm

But before we get too serious about anything, let's take a day off. They got a **rodeo** up in Pagosa on the Fourth every year. I'm thinkin' you'd really enjoy it. You're about due for a payday—maybe you could spend some of your earnin's. And I'd get a chance to take those hot mineral baths they got there. **Always does wonders for my bones.**"

Cloyd spent the afternoon riding Blueboy up the river and telling him the news about the mountains, over and over and over.

....

rodeo contest for ranchers

Always does wonders for my bones. They always make me feel better.

BEFORE YOU MOVE ON...

1. **Character's Point of View** Reread pages 99–100. How did Walter feel about Cloyd?

2. **Paraphrase** What did Walter mean on page 100 when he said, "the hurt you get over makes you stronger"?

LOOK AHEAD Read pages 103–108 to find out what Walter does to prepare for the trip.

12

Today was the big day. Cloyd and Walter had been up since four in the morning **shuttling** the packhorses, mining equipment, food, and camping gear to the trailhead at the end of the road up the Pine River. It was midafternoon, and thunderclouds were gathering over the mountains. On their third and last trip to the trailhead, they stopped in Bayfield to buy **a few last-minute supplies**. Walter bought a fishing rod for Cloyd, and hooks and salmon eggs. "**Used to be good fishing on the Pine**—bet it still is. If the trout don't like the salmon eggs, you can dig worms with the camp shovel or catch grasshoppers. Maybe you can catch us some fresh dinner now and again."

They drove up the river road. Cloyd could hardly

....

shuttling moving

a few last-minute supplies things they would need at the mine

Used to be good fishing on the Pine The Pine River was a good place to catch fish

believe he was finally going to the mountains. A few miles north, Walter **pulled off** by the Pine River Cemetery. He told Cloyd he could wait a few minutes or come along. Cloyd looked in on the saddle horses in the gooseneck trailer, Blueboy, and the old man's sorrel mare, while Walter walked into the little cemetery. Then he **caught up with the old man** in front of a pair of graves.

At the far end of the plot was centered a single stone. Cloyd recognized the name *Landis*. Underneath there were two names, and one of them was Walter's.

"Why is your name on this?" Cloyd asked **in undisguised confusion**.

Walter scratched the thick white bristles of his beard. It was almost grown out again. "All they have to do is put the date on. Makes it easy."

Cloyd picked dandelions and piled the flowers on the grass. He thought about Walter in a box under the grass. "Do you have any relatives?"

"**There's a few still around.** My brother's on the Animas River down in New Mexico, and my wife's kin are back in Missouri."

....

pulled off stopped the car
caught up with the old man walked to where Walter was
in undisguised confusion because he didn't understand
There's a few still around. Some of my family members are still alive.

Suddenly the wind began to blow. Cloyd looked up from the gravestones and saw the black clouds racing toward them from the mountains, where lightning flashed and rain hung in dark layers. He was chilled in his T-shirt, but he wanted to hear Walter talk. "Are people still alive after they die—like they say?"

"I don't know, really. Lots of folks believe there's life after death, but nobody knows for sure. Maybe your life is all there is. But that's plenty, ain't it? Make it good while you have it, is what I think, in case there ain't nothin' extra."

"Live in a good way. That's what my grandmother says."

"That's a fine way to put it."

The clouds **overtook them** and darkened the Pine River Valley. Thunder rumbled more frequently. A long bolt of lightning struck a few miles upriver, the **concussion and unraveling** thunder following behind. "Comin' our direction," Walter remarked with some anxiety.

Cloyd didn't want to cut off this talk with the old man.

....

"That's a fine way to put it." "I like the way she said that."

overtook them covered the sun above them

concussion and unraveling sound and movement of

It was important. They could always run for the truck.

"How come you stopped here—to talk to your wife?"

"Well, in a way. To tell her I'm goin' back to the mine, I guess."

"But she can't hear you."

"Prob'ly not, but it's more a matter of respect."

"How do you mean?"

"Showin' honor for her. I wouldn't do something this important without **consulting her** if she was alive. Matter of fact," he chuckled, "I wouldn't be doing it at all. But seeing the circumstances, she won't mind. She'd say, 'You go up there with Cloyd to that mine of yours and find your gold.'"

"But she isn't alive."

"**No, that ain't right.** Somehow, as long as I'm alive, she is, too."

"Like she's a part of you?"

"People get like that, Cloyd. That's what's special about people."

The wind stopped abruptly, and Walter had that **claustrophobic** feeling he got when the air pressure was

....

consulting her talking with her
No, that ain't right. That is not true.
claustrophobic closed in

106

dropping fast around him. "Say, **we better shake a leg**," he said, and turned from the grave.

The old man wasn't much for running, but he **shuffled** along as **briskly** as he could. They were barely inside the truck when the wind and the rain struck. "Let's **wait her out**," Walter said. "No sense driving in this."

Cloyd reached into his jeans pocket and pulled out the bearstone, set it on the dashboard. "I want to tell you a secret about this," he said.

Walter **appraised** the stone up close, the turquoise bear he'd nearly destroyed in anger. "It's some piece," he said. "Forehead's dished out like a grizzly's, and this bulge here on the back, it's almost like it's a hump."

"I found it with one of the Ancient Ones—a baby—in those rocks up there, above your farm."

"In the cliffs? A burial? Why, if that ain't somethin'."

"Bears are special for Ute people—they bring strength and good luck."

"All the more reason you've got yourself something special here," Walter said. "Think how old this stone must be. This blue bear's a real treasure, Cloyd."

....

we better shake a leg we should leave now

shuffled ran

briskly quickly

wait her out wait until the storm is over

appraised looked at

"When I found this, I gave myself a secret name. The Utes used to do that—they kept it secret except for one other person. You're the only one I'll ever tell my secret name to. It's Lone Bear. That's what it is— Lone Bear."

Walter **conjectured** what it might mean, the name Cloyd had taken for himself. It seemed like an awfully lonesome name. He wondered if the turquoise piece would bring the good luck the boy was hoping for.

"You know, Cloyd, some of that good luck just might **rub off on** the Pride of the West."

....

conjectured thought about
rub off on help us at

BEFORE YOU MOVE ON...

1. **Summarize** Reread page 106. Why did Walter go to his wife's grave before going to the mine?

2. **Inference** Why did Cloyd tell Walter about the bearstone and his secret name?

LOOK AHEAD Cloyd finally gets to visit the high country. Read pages 109–116 to find out how he feels.

Cloyd and Walter arrive at the mountains.
Cloyd fishes for the first time. When a storm
comes, Cloyd's life is suddenly in danger.

13

Walter **roused** Cloyd when it was still dark in their
camp at the **trailhead**. By the light of the gas lantern they
set to work sorting their gear into eight loads for the eight
packhorses. After sunrise Cloyd brought the horses into
camp from the meadow by the river where they'd been
hobbled overnight.

The packhorses stamped their feet and shied from the
wooden frames lifted toward them. **The packing dragged
on** all morning. Cloyd could hardly believe all the gear
they were taking with them. Two groups of backpackers
left up the trail while they were working. Finally the last
knot was tied, the riding horses saddled. Cloyd and Walter
led their animals to the wooden gate between the parking

....

roused woke up
trailhead beginning of the trail
set to work started
hobbled tied up
The packing dragged on They packed

lot and the beginning of the trail.

"What's this sign say?" Cloyd asked.

"Weminuche Wilderness Area. No motorized vehicles **beyond this point**."

Cloyd looked up the trail and saw it climb through a dense stand of pines. The trunks weren't far enough apart to allow even a jeep through. "Why do they have to say that?" he asked.

"Why, that means motorbikes, I suppose, and snowmobiles in the winter. Good thing, too. Our horses are **spooky enough without having to contend with motors**. That 'Weminuche' there, that's the name of the Utes who used to live up here."

"I know. My grandmother said that's us. We're the Weminuche."

"Well, now ain't that somethin'."

And then they were under way, each leading a **string** of four packhorses. Walter rode in front on his sorrel mare; Cloyd followed on the big blue roan.

The canyon soon narrowed, and the trail climbed well above the river. Cloyd found himself looking down hundreds of feet into pools so clear he could see the stones

....

beyond this point can ride past this sign
spooky enough without having to contend with motors scared easily even when they do not hear motors
string group

on the bottom. Above them, rockslide paths fell through the spruce and aspen forests from the peaks. As high as they were, these peaks weren't the towering, jagged ones he'd seen from the cliffs that first day at the farm. Before long, he would stand on top of one of the very highest and look out over the world.

The farther they worked their way up the Pine, the more Cloyd marveled at the steady gait and surefootedness of the roan. And when the horse had a chance, he'd **swivel** his eye back around and **catch sight of** the boy. There was something Cloyd had been **turning over and over in his mind** and now, he decided, was the time to ask the old man about it. "Is it true, like he said, that horses don't care anything about you?"

The old man hitched himself up in the saddle and halfway turned around. "You mean like Rusty said? **Don't pay no mind to his talk.** He just hates to agree with anybody. It's just the way he is."

"But is it true?"

"I've always puzzled on that, same as you. Horses appreciate good treatment and a steady hand, but it's a fact they don't go out of their way to fetch your slippers.

....

swivel turn
catch sight of look at
turning over and over in his mind thinking about a lot
Don't pay no mind to his talk. Do not listen to him.

Maybe some really do care. I've had one or two that made me think so, but it seems like you never know for sure. What do you think?"

"Oh, I was just wondering."

Cloyd was mostly disappointed with the old man's answer. As they rode, he continued to turn it over in his mind. He leaned forward and patted the roan. "Blueboy," he thought, "you're **not just any horse**. You and me, Blue, you and me."

The roan rolled an eye back and snorted loudly.

The next day the horses **labored** up ever-steeper grades as the river fell in leaps from the high country. Cloyd watched his string carefully as they crossed the tricky **scree** slides of fine rock that ran below them all the way to the river. Several times during the day they **forded** swift creeks that fed the Pine; with little urging, the roan crossed them easily. The others behind accepted his leadership.

Late in the afternoon they climbed out the canyon onto a large meadow, astonishingly green with knee-high grass and ringed by mountains that stabbed far above the

....

not just any horse different from other horses
labored climbed
scree dirt
forded crossed

line where the trees stopped growing. A small stream here close to the Continental Divide, the Pine River wound quietly in delicate **meanders** through the meadow. Walter said they'd **lay over** a day or two before they went up Snowslide Canyon to the mine. Cloyd was happy to **make camp**. As he'd been riding, he'd seen the trout darting through the **riffles** between the pools. They set up the sheepherder tent in the trees at the meadow's edge.

At first light Cloyd was up digging worms in the black soil underneath the trees. On the meadow, he sneaked up on a pool and let his bait drift into a likely spot. In a moment the rod came alive in his hands, and he launched the flashing trout into the air and over his head. A large cutthroat trout in its orange-red colors lay gasping in the grass. It was the first fish he'd ever caught and the beginnings of a meal for him and the old man. He remembered his grandmother saying that when the Weminuche lived in the mountains, some of the men were so skilled that they could catch fish with **their bare** hands. That didn't seem possible. But now he knew how they must have felt when they caught the lightning-fast trout,

....

meanders little streams
lay over stay here
make camp stop and make a place to stay
riffles little waves
their bare only their

however they did it.

Midway up the meadow Cloyd caught his second trout, and then his third at the upper end where the stream came rushing out of the trees. He'd discovered the fishing was better if he kept trying new water than if he stayed with one hole, even if he could see plenty of trout there. It seemed they would **strike** pretty quick, or not at all. He decided to look upstream in the trees for another good place to fish. After walking around the rapids through a thick spuce forest, he found an even bigger, more promising meadow above.

As Cloyd began to fish the upper meadow, white clouds boiled up out of the blue sky and quickly turned dark. The wind started to blow, but he was too excited to notice the wind or the clouds—he was **landing** trout. Several miles from camp, at the far end of the upper meadow, he caught his seventh. As he slid the new-caught fish onto the stringer he'd **fashioned** from a willow branch, he shook with cold and realized the temperature had been dropping for some time. He'd been out fishing longer than he thought. Without the sun it was hard to **judge the time**, but it could be past noon already. He saw

....

strike come to get the bait
landing catching
fashioned made
judge the time know what time it was

the clouds spill down the mountainsides toward him, dark and loaded with moisture. A few more pools, maybe one more fish, and he would collect his trout and **head for camp**.

Lightning broke loose and thunder rumbled, not too far off. A cold wind rushed down the meadow. He wished he'd worn more than a T-shirt, but he hadn't thought he would be **out long**. He knew he'd better run for it; the storm was about to break. As he picked up his stringer and started out, lightning cracked barely upstream. The shock wave and his surprise threw him to the ground. Glancing back, he saw the big spruces bending under the weight of the wind, and hail angling down with terrific speed.

Cloyd thought he could race the hail into the trees between the meadows and nestle in under a good roof of branches. He ran for the trees with the rod held high in his right hand and the stringer of trout in his left. He ran with a laughing heart because the hail was already pounding the meadow behind him, and yet at full speed he would outrun it just in time.

With no warning his right leg sank to the hip, his chest and face struck the ground, the rod and stringer of

....

head for camp walk back to camp

out long gone for a long time

With no warning his right leg sank to the hip Suddenly he fell

fish flew. In the tall grass, he'd failed to see the narrow trench connecting the stream with the pond where beavers had built one of their **domed lodges**.

Pain **coursed** through and through his leg. He was sure he'd hurt it badly. With his weight on his left knee, Cloyd dragged the right leg out of the beaver run and lay on his left side, watching the wall of hail advance down the meadow. He had to wait for the pain to clear. Lightning ripped the meadow simultaneously with its **deafening** thunder. A heartbeat later the hail struck, stinging him and bouncing all around in the grass. Within seconds he was drenched and started to shake with cold. His T-shirt and jeans clung to him; they offered no protection. The feeling went out of his fingers. He lay **motionless**, unable to think.

....

domed lodges homes
coursed went
deafening loud
motionless without moving

BEFORE YOU MOVE ON...

1. **Conclusions** How did Cloyd feel in the mountains? How can you tell?

2. **Inference** Reread page 111. Why do you think Cloyd asked if horses care about people?

LOOK AHEAD Cloyd falls and is hurt. Read pages 117–124 to find out how he gets help.

In minutes the meadow was carpeted with a layer of hail. All of a sudden, it was winter. Cloyd had seen hailstorms in the high desert, but not like this one. Here the air itself had turned freezing cold. Shaking now from fear as well as cold, he forced himself to think. **Managing another hundred yards to the trees meant nothing now.** He had to reach camp, the old man, and a fire—or freeze to death. He tried the leg. It could take some of his weight. Nothing was broken.

Cloyd knew he had to start out immediately, but somehow it seemed important not to leave the rod and the fish behind. They couldn't be far. As he raked through the hail-flattened grass with his sneakers, he realized he couldn't feel his feet. There was the rod. He scooped it up and clamped his fingers around it. Lucky for him it wasn't broken. And here were the trout, **stiff and staring**.

Then he ran as best he could, shaking, tripping, falling. The hail turned to cold and steady rain. Something told him that he **had no chance in** the woods, the way he came up from the lower meadow. He had to find a trail. Was there a trail? He hadn't seen one all day.

....

Managing another hundred yards to the trees meant nothing now. He had to walk with the hurt leg.

stiff and staring dead

had no chance in couldn't get through

Maybe there would be one on the far side of the meadow, across the stream.

Cloyd couldn't feel the icy water as he plunged across the Pine River holding up his rod and reel and his fish. In fact, he'd stopped shaking and couldn't feel anything at all. His body was getting too cold, much too cold.

Across the meadow he found a trail and **hastened** wildly down it. After a while he was in the trees. The trail fell sharply, muddy and slick, turning this way and that. He **veered through** dark shapes as if in a dream. No sign of the lower meadow and the old man, and the cold was squeezing the life out of him. Through the dark trees, off the trail and down by the stream, **a small patch of orange caught his eye**. His mind dismissed the image, but as he stumbled forward, the idea of the orange color slowly worked its way to the surface. It was a tent. Cloyd stopped and stared through the trees at a trace of blue smoke hanging in the dark branches above the tent.

He could barely move. It took him a long time to reach the orange tent. Now he stood dumbly by the remains of a fire. There was no fire here, only a bit of blue smoke

....

hastened hurried

veered through ran past

a small patch of orange caught his eye he saw something orange curling around the soggy stub of a log.

Cloyd faced the tent. "I need help," he said thickly.

Someone lifted the tent flap—a young man with glasses and a dark beard—and cursed in surprise. The man came out of the tent, took away the rod and the fish, and forced him to the ground and inside the small orange tent. Cursing softly, the man said not to worry. He rummaged through a sack, muttering something about **long johns**.

The man with the beard pulled Cloyd's wet clothes off. The boy looked curiously at his own body. It didn't seem to belong to him. He noticed he wasn't shaking anymore. He didn't even feel cold. Then the man was dressing him in different clothes. It took a long time. His elbows kept poking the tent. Everything was orange, orange all around.

The bearded man **stuffed** Cloyd into a sleeping bag and asked if he felt warmer. He couldn't even answer. Then he was alone. The man had left. The cold and the quiet crept into one another comfortably. The world went dark; he felt himself falling asleep. He drifted deeper and deeper into the dark, like a leaf settling into the bottom of a deep pool. It was almost perfectly peaceful. He was so

....

long johns warm underclothes
stuffed put

close to that perfect sleep **when something intruded, one faraway nagging detail**. He couldn't even tell what it was. After a while it was some kind of noise, very far away. A magpie or a raven squawking, or possibly even his sister come looking for him in the canyons and calling again and again. Yes, it was a human voice after all, nagging, calling, insisting, shouting, but it wasn't his sister. Gradually, **light seeped into his eyes**, and he saw a man with glasses and a black beard. Who was he?

The world was moving. No, he was moving, being dragged outside the orange tent into the dark trees, sleeping bag and all.

The man's glasses were fogged up. The man lay alongside him on his elbows blowing on the wet wood, making smoke. Some coals were glowing. The man kept **wheezing** on them. Finally they burst into a flame and the man placed a little stick across the flame and left again.

Branches were breaking somewhere. The tiny flame was gone. The man was back with his arms full of wood, and then he was on his elbows again, blowing until his face turned purple. The flame came back. The wood

....

when something intruded, one faraway nagging detail but something was bothering him

light seeped into his eyes he saw light

wheezing breathing

started to **catch**. The man left; branches were breaking. After a time he was back piling branches over the fire and blowing it into stronger and stronger flames. The flames grew brighter, bigger, stronger than the rain dripping from the trees.

The bearded man with fogged-up glasses was pulling him from the sleeping bag, standing him up close to the fire, arms locked around his chest. He could begin to feel the fire spreading warmth into his body. "You're going to be all right," the man was saying. Cloyd struggled to get free of the sleeping bag. The man unzipped it, let it fall, and gained a new hold on him. Cloyd struggled again. "Hang on there," the man cautioned, "you're still **medium rare**. I'm gonna **cook you until you're charbroiled**."

Finally Cloyd's eyes cleared, and the man **turned him loose**. He could stand by the fire on his own. The man went for more wood. After many trips he'd built a **bonfire**. At its edge he boiled water in an aluminum pan and made coffee. When Cloyd drank it, he warmed from

....

catch burn

medium rare cold

cook you until you're charbroiled keep you near the fire until you are warm

turned him loose stopped holding him up

bonfire big fire

the inside out and at last became as warm as he could want to be.

"Think I'll clean your fish, if you don't mind," the man said. "They'd make a great hot meal for you, better than my freeze-dried stuff. You just stay by the fire there and make some more coffee if you like."

Cloyd nodded. The man went away through the trees to clean the fish at the stream. After he'd been gone some time, Walter rode into camp in his yellow rainslicker, leading the roan.

"**Thank goodness** you're okay, Cloyd," he said softly.

Walter's eyes took in the oversized clothes that weren't the boy's, a bruise below the right eye, a long scratch on his neck, the jeans and T-shirt drying by the fire. "I've been everywhere. I was afraid I wouldn't find you."

"I caught seven fish," Cloyd said.

The stranger came back with the fish cleaned and neatly arranged on the willow-branch stringer. Walter drank coffee with him and **pieced together** what had happened. Cloyd tended the frying trout.

The young man gave Cloyd a poke. "You must crave the taste of trout, the way you hung onto 'em."

....

Thank goodness I am glad
Walter's eyes took in Walter looked at
pieced together heard

A shy smile brightened the boy's face. "I guess so," he said.

Nothing ever tasted so warm or so good, Cloyd thought, as the three of them shared the fish. Except maybe new-made frybread.

Cloyd saw the worry finally leaving the old man's face. It seemed like the time to explain how he could have been so stupid. "I could have found a dry place in the trees, but I was running and fell into a hole."

The old man winked at the stranger and chuckled. "**From the looks of it,** the ground flew up and hit you in the face."

They all laughed. Cloyd pulled on his T-shirt and jeans. Not only dry, they were almost too hot for comfort. Walter went to his mare and pulled Cloyd's denim jacket from his saddlebags. Cloyd **dismantled** the fishing rod, then stood by the fire, turning his hands over even though they were warm already. He wanted to say something to the young man. He wouldn't have a chance to show it like with Walter. "Thank you," he said. Their eyes met for a moment. "You didn't have to . . . you didn't even know me, and you—"

....

From the looks of it, It looks like
dismantled took apart

"**No big deal**," the stranger said quickly. **"You'd have done the same for me."**

....

No big deal You don't need to thank me

"You'd have done the same for me." "You would have helped me if I needed it."

BEFORE YOU MOVE ON...

1. **Cause and Effect** Why did Cloyd have problems getting back to camp?

2. **Character** Reread pages 62 and 119. How had Cloyd changed?

LOOK AHEAD Read pages 125–134 to find out how Walter and Cloyd feel about the mine.

Walter tells Cloyd about grizzly bears. When they get to the mine, Walter is excited to begin work. Cloyd starts to worry about the mine.

14

For two days they rested in their campsite by the meadow. **When Cloyd recovered his strength, they set out for the mine.** Past the upper meadow where Cloyd had been caught by the cloudburst, Walter reined in his mare and motioned the boy and his string of packhorses alongside. "That canyon there," he pointed, indicating a steep-sided cleft in the mountains across the river, "that's Snowslide. The Pride of the West is **on up it a ways.** Won't be long now."

They forded the river and angled away from it up Snowslide Creek. Cloyd took a last look up the Pine River and knew at once he'd found what he'd been looking

....

When Cloyd recovered his strength, they set out for the mine. When Cloyd felt better, they went to the mine.

on up it a ways up that canyon

for. A single peak rising alone and high above the others had just come into view, a sharp peak riding alone in the turquoise sky. "What's that?" he called to the old man. "That mountain over there."

"That one yonder? Why, that's the Rio Grande Pyramid. Looks like one, don't it? That's where the Rio Grande River gets started—flows off the other side. That's quite a mountain, all right. Supposed to have been a grizzly and two cubs sighted on it about ten years ago."

"Grizzly bears?"

"That's right. Used to be plenty in this country, but that was some years ago. Of course we still have black bears."

"But this man saw three grizzly bears?"

"Says they was huntin' **marmots** just above the tree line. Most folks think he saw a big cinnamon, which is a black bear when he's brown. The last grizzly bear proven in the state of Colorado—or south of Wyoming, for that matter—was killed near here in 1954. It's on display in a museum up in Denver."

Cloyd **fingered** the smooth bearstone in his pocket. He wondered if it might really represent a grizzly, as Walter had suggested. He remembered that the old Utes

....

marmots small animals
fingered touched

especially honored grizzlies. "Do *you* think there's any more grizzly bears?" he asked.

"Don't know—most likely not. It's been a bunch of years since that fellow saw 'em, if that's what they were. But if he was right, and nobody's killed 'em since, the cubs'd be **in their prime** now."

"Do you think somebody probably killed them?"

"Not that anybody's heard about. But if a fellow was to kill one, he might not **let on** since they're protected now."

"What's that mean, 'protected'?"

"**On account of being** endangered. That means there's so few of 'em that if anybody kills one, there might be none left, so it's against the law."

For several hours they rode up Snowslide Canyon, crossing many of the wide, grassy paths among the sun-whitened hulks of spruces ripped from the edges of the slides high above. At the bottom of one of the avalanche chutes, the old man and the boy found a big log and set out biscuits and canned pork for their midday meal. Walter pointed out the knee-high trees dotting the grassy route of the slide. "When they get just a bit bigger, the

....

in their prime big and strong
let on say he had killed a grizzly bear
On account of being The grizzly bears are protected because they are

slide'll knock 'em down. They never quit trying, though. It's like building your house on a railroad track."

Scanning the skyline, the old man looked upstream. A smile crossed his face as he pointed up the canyon. "That peak with the ledge around the top like a crown sits directly above the mine. **My tunnel's aimin' for** the contact in the solid-gold heart of the mountain. The Pride of the West."

Cloyd thought about a heart made out of solid gold. It sounded like an awful cold heart. He didn't say so. "What's the contact?" he asked.

"A fissure vein of ore is what it is. Ore's the rock the gold is in. You see, gold is usually mixed with other minerals in veins that run through the mountain. If you find a good fissure vein, it'll never **give out on you** like a fault will. A fault leaves little pockets of ore called stringers. You find one of 'em, **dig it out**, and that's the end of it. But with a good fissure vein, you always have something to follow. Sometimes it'll narrow on you, maybe to inches, but then it'll widen out to eight feet or more."

My tunnel's aimin' for I built a tunnel to find
give out on you run out of gold
dig it out take out the gold

Cloyd realized he would actually be mining soon, inside a mountain in the dark. **Up to now he'd thought about it hardly at all.** At White Mesa most people thought of mining as a bad thing, though many of the men worked off and on in the mines or at the ore-shipping depot. The uranium made you get sick and die early, his grandmother said. She never said if gold made you sick. But then he remembered what she had said about gold. It made people crazy and dishonest. First the white men promised the Utes they could keep the mountains forever, but that was before gold was discovered and **the miners came pouring in**. The white men forgot all about their promise. The Utes were told to stay out of the mountains. They couldn't roam around anymore and live in the old way. They were given tiny reservations in the low country and told to stay there and grow corn.

"You really think there's gold in your mine?" he asked skeptically.

"Why, I know there is! I crossed a vein of silver already, but I didn't even bother to follow it, 'cause in those days silver wasn't worth much unless it was real high-grade ore. I got a three-hundred-foot tunnel in

....

Up to now he'd thought about it hardly at all. This was the first time he thought of it.

the miners came pouring in many men came to mine the gold

already, an' I figure from the geology there can't be more'n a few more to the contact. **I ain't really gambling**, Cloyd. Why, I already found the contact, you see, where the vein breaks the surface way up the mountain. It's tilted at a pretty good angle, and the idea of the tunnel is to reach it inside the mountain and then **stope up** to the surface."

"How come you didn't dig where you found it?"

"Sure wish I could have. But it's better mining sense to work upwards and let gravity move your rock for you—down ore chutes. It's too hard to move any quantity of rock uphill unless you've got heavy machinery."

The dubious cast to Cloyd's face told Walter he'd given the boy no feel for the joy of working in hard rock, the thrill of blasting and then returning to the drift always expecting to see a vein of high-grade ore laid open. "There's fabulous wealth in these mountains, Cloyd," he whispered **reverentially**. "And most of it hasn't been discovered yet. Let me tell you about the Cresson Mine up in the Cripple Creek District right here in Colorado. They were blastin' the face of the tunnel, following a

....

I ain't really gambling I know that there is gold

stope up make steps up

The dubious cast to Cloyd's face told Walter he'd given the boy no feel for the joy Walter could see from Cloyd's face that the boy did not know about the fun

reverentially seriously

fissure vein, and broke into a natural room forty feet long by twenty feet wide and fifteen feet high. A vug is what it was, like a geode—ever see a rock that's hollow in the middle with crystals all around? Well, this big room they found was a giant geode with the crystals sticking out the floor, the walls, the ceiling—everything was solid gold!"

It seemed from Walter's eyes that he was even now peering into the gold cave he'd described. Cloyd could see how much it meant to the old man. He would do his best for Walter, even though it sounded dark and cold and dangerous, and then he would climb the Rio Grande Pyramid for himself. "How much gold did they get from in there?" he asked politely, as the old man **came out of his reverie**.

"**I recollect** it was two and one-half million. At today's price—four hundred fifty dollars an ounce—that's be . . . thirty-some million dollars from that one room!"

They continued up the canyon until Walter stopped at a bend in the trail and stared across the creek where a great pile of tailings jutted from the mountainside. "The Pride of the West," Walter whispered. "It took me nearly forty years to get back, but I finally **made it**. And my

....

came out of his reverie stopped dreaming about the mines
I recollect I remember
made it came back

goodness, it doesn't look a bit different. Mountains don't get old very fast, Cloyd. This mountain, it's like it blinked while I went off a young man, looks again and sees me ridin' back **plumb aged**."

Walter and Cloyd set up the big sheepherder tent by the stream under a tall cluster of spruce. Once they had unpacked all the horses, they hobbled them in the grass across the creek where only a few rotted logs remained of the old man's corral. Then they climbed up the side of the ore dump and gained the landing on top, only to discover raw earth where the mine entrance should have been.

"Well, she's caved in, and not so long ago," Walter said, disappointed yet calm. "Just the **portal**, Cloyd. The topsoil slipped, is all. Inside it'll be fine, once we move this dirt out of the way. It's all hard rock once you're inside—we'll be in there drillin' in a few days."

"Drilling?" Cloyd asked vacantly. For a moment he'd hoped Walter would **give it all up**.

"Makin' holes in the rock—pretty deep—so we can slip the dynamite in and blast. We're going to have to do our drillin' the old way, with one of us holding the bit and the other pounding the sledgehammer. **Slow going**,

....

plumb aged as an old man
portal entry
give it all up decide not to work in the mine
Slow going It is slow

but it works. They quit drilling by hand in the 1870s, way before my time. After that, doublejackin'—that's two men working like I said—was only for drilling contests or for fellows like me that didn't know any better mining back in the hills where you couldn't use machine drills. Drillin's hard work—can be dangerous, too."

"Dangerous?"

"One story I remember, there was these two men working high up on **a scaffold** in a big room inside a mine, and they were double-jackin' into the face up there. Must've been twenty-five feet up they was standing. Of a sudden their scaffolding **busts**, and the one doing the sledgework, he crashes down with it. Now his partner turning the bit, he grabs hold of his **steel** as he's falling, and it's stuck good and stout in the hole, so there he is hanging from it pretty as you please. He starts hollerin' for help of course, only his buddy's got nothing to help him with, and there's nobody else around. So after about five minutes, the fellow up above can't hold on no longer, and he crashes down, too. His buddy says, 'Dang—I knew you was slow, but I had no idea it'd take you five minutes to fall twenty-five feet!'"

....

a scaffold a floor built to stand on; a platform
busts breaks
steel tool

"Is that a true story?"

"Yes sir, that's a true story," the old man said as he stroked the bristles on his chin. But quickly his ears turned red and his cheeks puffed in and out as he tried to hold his breath and keep from laughing.

"True?" Cloyd repeated gravely.

Walter's cheeks collapsed and his breath exploded. "True . . . and then some," he said, slapping his knees.

Cloyd had to laugh, too. It was good to be laughing with the old man.

....

Walter's cheeks collapsed and his breath exploded. Walter laughed.

BEFORE YOU MOVE ON...

1. **Cause and Effect** Reread page 129. Why did Cloyd think mining was bad?

2. **Comparisons** What did the trip to the mountains mean to Cloyd? What did it mean to Walter?

LOOK AHEAD Read pages 135–140 to find out how hard it is to work in a gold mine.

Cloyd and Walter start to work in the mine.
Walter wants to work all of the time, but he
sees that Cloyd is unhappy.

15

It took three days of **tedious handwork for them to clear the entrance**. At last Cloyd's shovel broke through into empty space. He knelt and looked through the small opening. He saw only blackness but felt a steady flow of cool air escaping the mine through the hole he'd made. "Where's the air coming from?" he asked Walter.

"Oh, that's one of the lucky things about this mine—fresh air's always moving through it. Comes down from the surface through cracks in the **formations**."

Once they'd completely cleared the portal, Walter showed Cloyd how to **rig his headlamp** and how to **ignite**

....

tedious handwork for them to clear the entrance hard and boring work to move the rocks away from the opening

formations rocks in the mountain

rig his headlamp use the flashlight on his hard hat

ignite light

the gas that came from the water dripping on the **carbide**. Then they started inside.

As they ventured down the center of the narrow railway, the air felt pleasantly cool. Cloyd glanced constantly over his shoulder to the blinding white light of the portal; he banged his hard hat against a tooth of rock in the low ceiling. The cold surprised him, **suddenly finding** his bones. Next time he'd wear his sweatshirt and jacket. At the end of the tunnel, he was surprised by the **ore car**, big enough that both of them could have climbed in. "How'd you get this thing up here?" he asked.

"Oh, I had to take it apart with the torch and whatnot, machine new parts for bolting it back together, bring it in pieces up here on horseback, then reassemble it. **The rails were somethin' else again.**"

In the morning they entered the mine ready for work. Cloyd held tight to the heavy drill bits and the long copper spoons. The one thing he liked was the feel of the hard hat and the hiss of burning gas in his headlamp. Before long, he told himself, he'd be accustomed to the strangeness

....

carbide metal

suddenly finding and he felt it in

ore car cart that carried rocks in the mine

The rails were somethin' else again. It was hard to put the rails together, too.

inside the mountain. Working with the old man he wouldn't be so afraid of being trapped in the dark under the earth. At the end of the tunnel, Walter pointed out the vein of silver ore he'd been following many years before on his way to the gold contact. Cloyd was surprised to find it wasn't silver-colored at all, but black, peppered here and there in the quartz.

"Now set those spoons and drills down," Walter said. "I'll tell you how we're going to start. We'll drill seven lucky holes in a circle around this vein, then three in the center about two feet apart in a triangle, anglin' 'em so they meet inside like the top of a pyramid."

"Then the dynamite?"

"Not yet. We drill a reliever at the top of the face, edgers on both sides, and a lifter at the bottom. If we do it right, we **time the charges** so the center comes out first, making space so's everything around it has somewhere to go when it's blasted **a hair later**. The lifter going last kicks it all out where we can **muck** it into the ore car."

"What do I do?"

"You're my partner when we're double-jackin'. That's one man working the drill bit, the other the

....

time the charges calculate when the dynamite explodes

a hair later a little while later

muck move, empty

sledgehammer. We'll stop every so often and fish out the dust with the spoons."

"How fast can we go?" Cloyd asked with little hope.

"Not fast at all. **But what's time to a hog?** I'll tell you what a good **pace** would be, though, so you know what those old-timers could do. A good pair of double-jackers could drill two inches a minute if they were going all out. Over a longer run, like an hour, they'd go maybe thirty inches."

"Why can't we?"

"We've got to **play it safe**. We're two days from help. Those drill heads make a mighty small target for a sledgehammer. Once I saw a Fourth of July drillin' contest up in Silverton that really made an impression on me— now this is a true story. The object of the competition was to see how deep you could drill in fifteen minutes. These two bull-strong Cornishmen took their turn havin' at a six-foot-thick **slab of Gunnison granite**. The man on the sledge, early on in the contest, he's working at a good fifty-blow-per-minute pace. Of a sudden we see his hammer

....

But what's time to a hog? But we do not need to worry about time.

pace speed

play it safe work safely

slab of Gunnison granite piece of rock

stopped up in the air. We realize he's just hit his partner's hand, and the crowd groans, but the hurt man yells, 'Bring it down! Bring it down!'"

"What did that mean?"

"He didn't want to quit even though he'd been hurt bad. So the sledgeman resumes hammering. We see the hand go red, the man's face showin' **it's all he can do to keep the bit turning**. His blood is mixing with the water flushin' out the dust. Every time the hammer comes down, the crowd is splashed with bloody water. Then it's time for the hurt man to take his turn with the sledge, and still he won't quit. When the hammer's up in the air, the blood runs down his arm until it's red all the way to the shoulder. That man never **gave up** until the timer gave the signal. Then he fainted dead away."

"He died?"

"No—blacked out."

"Did they win?"

"No," Walter said thoughtfully, "they didn't come close. But they finished. Couldn't pay men to do that no more. Then again, there's fools like us doing it for free!"

To Cloyd it all seemed impossibly strange and

---

it's all he can do to keep the bit turning he's doing everything he can to continue

gave up stopped working

dangerous. But he would work. If he worked as hard as he had making the fenceline, he wouldn't feel the strangeness or the danger. And this time he'd trust in the old man and not **blow up** like before.

....

blow up get angry

BEFORE YOU MOVE ON...

1. **Cause and Effect** Cloyd wanted to work fast, like he did on the fence. Why couldn't Cloyd and Walter work quickly at the mine?

2. **Character's Point of View** Reread page 139. What did Walter think about the miner in the story?

LOOK AHEAD Read pages 141–148 to find out how the gold mine changes Walter.

After seven days of bone-rattling drilling they were ready to blast. As Walter wished, Cloyd waited outside while he placed the dynamite in the drill holes and set the timing on the fuses.

Cloyd was exhausted. The cold had **sapped all his strength**. The work had been repetitive, painful, endless. In a pretty place he could enjoy working; in the mine **he'd endured it only for the sake of the old man**. At first they'd taken long breaks outside, down by the creek where they could lie in the grass, eat, and rest. But as the days went by, Walter **stretched the working hours** and made the breaks shorter. Close to the blasting, Cloyd could tell the old man didn't want to break at all or even sleep. He was so excited, he wanted to work through to the end to see what he would find.

At last all was ready. Walter came out of the mine to make sure Cloyd was standing **well clear of** the portal, then went back inside to set off the charges. After awhile he came running out of the tunnel with a wild look in his eye, and yelled, "Fire in the hole! Fire in the hole!"

Cloyd smiled. The expression on the old man's

....

sapped all his strength made him tired
he'd endured it only for the sake of the old man he only did it because it was important to Walter
stretched the working hours made them work more
well clear of far from

face made it all worthwhile. Then came the waves of **concussion as the charges** rumbled inside the mine and dark clouds of smoke and dust poured out the entrance.

It was some time before the air cleared enough for them to reenter the mine. Cloyd was surprised to see how little progress the blast had made. No more than four feet. Walter knelt and examined piece after piece of the rock freed by the explosion. He'd hoped there might be at least some good silver ore for them to take home, but he was disappointed. "**Poor makin's**," he said. "Weak silver. Not even worth packing out for **assay**."

They had nothing to show for their long days, Cloyd thought. But then, he'd never really believed they'd find anything. Now they'd have to shovel all the broken rock into the car and drop it over the edge of the dump outside. It would take many loads to clear out the tunnel for work on the next round. Yet Walter turned to the hand-mucking with new enthusiasm. "Next time we'll **turn up** something better," he said. "We're after gold anyway. You talk to that lucky bear of yours. This is still a promising vein, and silver can lead to gold."

....

concussion as the charges sound as the explosions
Poor makin's I did not find anything good
assay metal
turn up find

Cloyd was convinced they were wasting their time, but he said nothing. He'd been trying to hide his feelings from the old man. Somehow there hadn't been any time for him to go fishing. Somehow, after the first few nights, there was no time set aside to sit around the campfire in the evenings. There'd only been time to work, eat, and sleep.

Shovelful by weary shovelful, he helped Walter muck out the tunnel. The bigger rocks he had to **grapple** with and lift by hand. Once the ore car was finally filled, they had to wedge its wheels to a stop every few feet, or it would speed out of control and **hurtle** over the dump down to the creek.

Each night, he'd noticed, the cold seemed to bite a little deeper. The fragile high-country summer was beginning to lose out to winter. **He fretted that he was losing his chance at the peaks.** It took them a whole day to clear the mine. The prospect of starting all over again on the next round of drilling was worse than the work itself. Six or seven more days of **spine-wracking torment to endure** before they'd be ready to blast again.

....

grapple struggle

hurtle fall

He fretted that he was losing his chance at the peaks. He worried that he would not have time to climb the mountains.

spine-wracking torment to endure very difficult work to do

Before long, he knew too well, they'd have to leave the mountains, and then school would start. His precious time in the mountains was being used to take the inside of one apart and move it outside. He was trying hard, but he wasn't sure he'd be able to **hold up**.

Three, four, five days of the second **go-round** passed. Cloyd **worked in a trance**, trying to concentrate on turning the bit between blows. There was only the penetrating cold and the hiss of burning acetylene in his headlamp, the numbing feel of cold steel in his hands, the stinging shock of the blow, and the harsh **reports** of the hammer rattling up and down the confines of the mine. It was enough to drive him crazy.

More and more, Walter **begrudged** himself the time it took to eat and sleep. He had to see what the next blast would turn up. He'd come up with fresh calculations and convinced himself he was closer than he'd thought to the contact, that artery of high-grade gold ore which would lead him directly to the heart of the mountain. His old obsession had taken over and he'd forgotten about the

....

hold up continue
go-round try
worked in a trance worked without thinking
reports sounds
begrudged didn't give

boy, about Cloyd's great desire to see the high country. He'd forgotten what he told Susan James, that the trip wasn't so much for the mining as the chance to introduce the boy to the mountains.

Though it had lain dormant for almost forty years, the great illness of his youth—gold fever—**had blossomed in its most virulent strain and invaded all his faculties**. He'd slipped into the assumption that their enterprise was as exciting for Cloyd as it was for himself. Until, that is, they neared the second round of blasting. In a moment of clarity during their midday break he **happened to read the boy's face**. He realized he'd made the boy a prisoner of sorts again and must set him free at once. But he had to do it in such a way that Cloyd wouldn't feel compelled to stay and help out. He himself had no intention of quitting with the contact so near.

A stratagem came to mind. Not one his wife would have approved of, or he either under ordinary circumstances. It deviated by a substantial margin from the truth. A white lie, he told himself, for the boy's benefit.

....

had blossomed in its most virulent strain and invaded all his faculties made it hard for Walter to think about anything other than gold

happened to read the boy's face saw how Cloyd felt

A stratagem came to mind. Walter thought of a plan.

"Well, Cloyd, **I've had it**," he said disgustedly.

Surprised, Cloyd looked up and saw the disappointment all across the old man's face. "How do you mean?" he asked.

"Like they say in the oil business, **it's a dry hole**. We're wasting our time."

"But you won't know until you blow it up again and see."

A logical objection, Walter thought. He'd have to counter with **bogus** expertise. "Oh, I've been looking at the powder we've been fishing out of the drill holes with those spoons. Indications are bad, mighty poor. I figure we ought to give it up before we shoot what's left of the summer. Didn't you want to climb one of these mountains, maybe that Rio Grande Pyramid?"

"Maybe the gold's just a little farther," Cloyd insisted.

"Maybe. But chances are slim to none. If we quit now we'll have a little time—maybe a week—before we have to head back. Now what about that Pyramid? Let's get you some food packed, go over some maps—why, you could be ready to take out in the morning."

....

I've had it I do not want to work in the mine anymore
it's a dry hole there is nothing to find here
bogus fake, made-up

"Aren't you coming with me?"

For a moment, Walter was so touched that Cloyd would want him along, he almost abandoned his plan. Though **he lacked the wind** for climbing at high altitude, they could ride together and set up a base camp before the boy set out alone. But even more he was **relishing** the next blast and the treasure it might **break loose**. "My lungs couldn't take the thin air," he said. "That's close to fourteen thousand feet. **I might have a fit or somethin'.**"

"We wouldn't have to go so high up."

"No, Cloyd, I'd rather stick close to camp here and just enjoy myself pokin' around, lookin' at the scenery, brewin' coffee and whatnot. You take Blueboy—you're better off on horseback as far as you can go. Take a packhorse, too. Park your horses in the trees before you climb up above timberline."

Suddenly Walter was spooked. He shouldn't be letting the boy go off alone in the mountains. It was never a good idea, no matter how experienced you were. Yet he'd done it often enough when he was young. "Stay off of those

....

he lacked the wind his breathing wasn't strong enough

relishing waiting eagerly for

break loose uncover

I might have a fit or somethin'. It might make me sick.

peaks when **the weather's comin' on**. You know what that's about."

"I'll be careful," Cloyd promised.

....

the weather's comin' on a storm comes

BEFORE YOU MOVE ON...

1. **Conclusions** How was Walter changed by "gold fever"?

2. **Character's Motive** Why did Walter send Cloyd to the mountains?

LOOK AHEAD Read pages 149–158 to see how Cloyd and Blueboy get into trouble.

Cloyd and Blueboy climb the mountain. After Blueboy gets hurt, Cloyd continues climbing alone.

16

Mile by mile Cloyd rode up the gentle meadows of the Pine. As he saw the Rio Grande Pyramid **gradually nearing**, his confidence grew. He rode with beauty all around him. He rode on a powerful horse who was his friend. "Hey-a, Blueboy, hey-a!"

Cloyd's spirit was free and had all the running room in the world. There was no limit to where it might go or what was possible. "Hey-a," he sang. "Hey-a, hey-a, Blueboy."

The roan tried to break into a trot, even into a run, but the packhorse held him back. Cloyd could tell that Blueboy **was taken with the morning's wild spirit; this day was made for the two of them**. He dismounted and tied the packhorse to a tree a little ways off the trail, and then he walked back to the roan and said, "Let's run, Blue, I mean really run."

....

gradually nearing getting closer
was taken with the morning's wild spirit loved feeling free
this day was made for the two of them it was the perfect day

And then they ran streaming through the meadows of the Pine. **Cloyd and the horse were one**, and they were flying through the wind and the light, while all around him shone the mountains and the trees and the river. Cloyd grinned as they ran, and then he **broke into a smile**. **His teeth caught the wind.** He couldn't stop smiling all the way up the meadow. This day was different. It was as if he was coming into a new world all bright and shining, and it was made for him.

They rested at the end of the meadow, and they drank from the stream. The roan was delighted with the meadow grass and tore at it as if he hadn't eaten for weeks. Cloyd lay on his back in the grass and watched the trees on the hillside sway in the wind. He wondered if trees could feel. He decided that they could. They liked to wrap themselves in the air, sway with the breeze, and let the air soothe their branches and every little needle.

Back on the horse, he leaned forward to speak. The roan swiveled an ear back. "Want to?" Cloyd whispered. "Want to, Blue?"

The roan **exploded into a gallop**, and they ran all

....

Cloyd and the horse were one Cloyd and Blueboy felt the same way

broke into a smile smiled happily

His teeth caught the wind. He felt the wind on his teeth.

exploded into a gallop ran quickly

the way back down the meadow. Then he collected the packhorse and continued on his way to the Pyramid. After several miles he had to leave the trail and **strike upward** through the dark spruce forest. There were no trails where he was going. Blueboy and the packhorse labored in the rapidly thinning air as Cloyd guided them through the deadfall. Up, up they climbed. After a few miles Cloyd rested them on a bench where waterfalls spilled into a string of beaver ponds. The horses grazed while Cloyd ate his lunch. **Contentment seeped through and through him.** This place was almost enough, he felt so good. The peak, if he made it, would be **surplus to store against** the future. He resolved to see as much of the mountains as he could. Besides the Pyramid, he was taken with two other names: Ute Lake and the Rincon La Osa, "the corner of the bear."

As he climbed again, the spruces huddled in clusters, squatter than they grew below, and grassy slopes led to a world of wildflowers. He left the last of the trees behind and rode through windblown waves of reds, yellows, and blues. He could almost reach out and touch

....

strike upward climb up

Contentment seeped through and through him. He felt happy and peaceful.

surplus to store against something extra special to make him strong in

the Continental Divide. That's where, as Walter had explained, rivers bound for different oceans started out **within spitting distance of** each other.

He rested the horses while he **took it all in**. Here he was in the high, treeless world patched with snowbanks as far as he could see, the spongy, delicate, windlashed birthplace of rivers. A lone giant, the Pyramid loomed above and only a few miles away. He wondered if it could really be climbed. Close at hand, a spectacular formation in the Divide **caught his fancy**. It was called the Window, and it was so close he could see birds flying in the wide gap between its sheer walls. They were small birds, and they seemed to be flying loops for the sheer joy of it. They come to play, he realized. The air must pour through there like anything.

He noticed a bit of an elk trail leading to the Window across the steep scree slides of fine rock. **On the spur of the moment** he said to the roan, "You want to stand in that Window, Blueboy? I sure do." He tied the packhorse and rode the roan toward the Window. He wanted to stand between those towering walls and feel the air

....

within spitting distance of right next to
took it all in looked around him
caught his fancy interested him
On the spur of the moment Suddenly

currents, see the birds up close, and look over the other side.

They started across the elk trail. Once out on the scree slope, Cloyd thought the elk that cross it must be very surefooted, or very brave. The fine rock slid under the roan's hoofs, and the steepness of the slope underneath them began to worry him. Maybe it's a mountain goat trail, he thought. Yet there was no place to turn around, no choice but to keep going forward.

They **inched across the dizzying** slope until they reached the Window, and then the roan **balked about going** up. "We're almost there," Cloyd encouraged him. Then he chuckled, and said, "Don't you want to stand on that windowsill?" With a jump, the roan **gained the rock ledge** and they were standing right where Cloyd wanted to be, in between those sheer walls like towers. He watched the **swallows put on a show**. He could even see the rainbow in their wing patches. To the north, across the Rio Grande country, a whole new world had opened up. It seemed like the wilderness had no end.

If only the old man could see us standing here, he

....

currents blowing
inched across the dizzying walked slowly on the high
balked about going did not want to go
gained the rock ledge landed on the high, flat rock
swallows put on a show birds fly

thought—me and Blueboy in the Window. I wish my sister could, my grandmother, and Susan James. But especially the old man. What a wonderful day, he thought. And there's not a cloud in the sky.

Cloyd thought about the Pyramid. There was still time to climb it today. Tomorrow the weather could turn bad.

He realized it would be harder for the roan to step off the windowsill than it had been to scramble up. He could fall. Besides, he liked the idea of riding *through* the Window, and so he did. He rode through, and then he looped one of the towers until he gained the ridgetop and **picked up a thread** of a trail. The slope was awful steep, but **it wasn't all scree** like the one he crossed before; there was quite a bit of grass on it. Halfway down, the roan **pulled up and held his ground**. In front of them, **a spring popped** out of the mountain and made a little **bog** on the slope. Cloyd didn't know why the roan wouldn't go across. The horse was looking around, but there was no passage above or below the muddy spot. "We don't mind the mud," Cloyd said. He smacked his lips and kicked the

....

picked up a thread found a part

it wasn't all scree it did not have loose rocks

pulled up and held his ground stopped and would not go on

a spring popped water came

bog wet area

horse forward. "C'mon, Blueboy, you can do it. You can do it, Blueboy."

The roan tried the mud and eased into it. Afterward, Cloyd remembered how the horse glanced back at him, as if for reassurance.

The roan took another step and was into the mud all the way up to one of his front shoulders. His other three legs were scrambling, scrambling desperately for footing, but the one leg was trapped, and Blueboy was falling.

In the moment the horse went down, it was all a blur. Cloyd knew only that he was about to be crushed. He barely managed to free his feet from the stirrups and to **lunge** uphill as the roan fell on its side.

Cloyd was **pinned** in the mud, and all around his head were the four hoofs of the roan. He saw the horseshoes and even the nails in the horseshoes.

Cloyd saw Blueboy tense and prepare to kick. The roan had to kick for balance, **to resist the pull of the slope underneath him**, and when he did, he'd crush the boy's skull. Cloyd thrashed with all his might to free himself, but he was completely **mired**.

....

lunge jump

pinned stuck, trapped

to resist the pull of the slope underneath him to keep from falling down the hill

mired stuck

Their eyes met, in a moment Cloyd would never forget. Blueboy was **poised** to kick, and then he saw Cloyd's head there, and then he didn't kick, not at all, but slowly, slowly, rolled over on his back. All four legs arced away from the boy, and then Blueboy tucked his legs in and tumbled down the mountain, slowly at first, then faster and faster like a **trundling** boulder.

The roan lay at the foot of the scree slope several hundred feet below. Full of dread, Cloyd freed himself from the mud and worked his way down to the horse. Blueboy was alive, but how badly hurt? His breathing came in spurts; he wasn't getting up. "Maybe you're okay," he told the horse, without believing it might be so. "Maybe you're okay. You gotta get up! Are your legs broken? Are you **all busted up inside**?"

Cloyd made the roan stand up. He was amazed to see Blueboy get up and then walk. He kept talking to the horse; he was so relieved and thankful. After a little while, he led Blueboy down to the tundra grass. Somehow, there were no broken bones, nothing to show but a few scratches. Somehow, they'd both lived through it. He led

....

poised ready
trundling rolling
all busted up inside hurt, injured

the horse down and around the base of the slope and back up to the packhorse.

Cloyd found a camp barely into the trees, by a trickle of a stream running off the snowbanks. There was no way he was going to try to climb the Pyramid this day. Brushing the dried mud off his clothes, he **marveled at the sacrifice his horse had made**. He shouldn't have taken Blueboy where he did. He wondered if he would climb the Pyramid at all; he wondered if he should even try. Maybe he should just get back to the old man while he was safe. He didn't really know what he was doing anyway. He'd almost killed the horse, could've got killed himself. What did he need to stand on the top of a mountain for anyway? Cloyd brooded through the long evening, finally crawled into his sleeping bag, and fell asleep by the fading fire. In his dreams, the horse kept falling over and over all night. He woke up, freezing in the cold night air. He should have **pitched** his tent. He wished the day would come.

At first light he woke, and he knew he couldn't ride away and give up, leave his dream behind. Maybe he would fail, but at least he had to try. Maybe what

....

marveled at the sacrifice his horse had made thought about what the horse did for him

pitched set up

happened with the roan was all a part of **earning** the peak, not a reason to give up. Hadn't the old man said that the hurt you get over makes you stronger?

....

earning working for the right to be on

BEFORE YOU MOVE ON...

1. **Cause and Effect** Why did Blueboy get hurt on the mountain? How could Cloyd have stopped the problem from happening?

2. **Plot** What sacrifice did Blueboy make for Cloyd? How did this make Cloyd feel?

LOOK AHEAD Does Cloyd reach the top of the Pyramid? Read to page 163 to find out.

He ate quickly and set out on foot. "Good-bye, Blueboy," he called over his shoulder. "I'm going for the top of the world."

Within a few hours he'd angled up the mountain far enough to **emerge from** the trees and find the Pyramid towering right in front of him. As yet not a cloud had formed over the mountains. Already he could see the mesas down in New Mexico. How much greater would be the view from the peak, where he would be able to see in all directions. **With spirits rising he bounded** from rock to rock on the **talus slopes tumbling** from the ridge high above. The small rockrabbits called pikas squeaked and scurried among the boulders on all sides. A marmot the size of a small dog stood on its hind legs and whistled shrilly at him. He grinned to think about how the old man called them whistle pigs. "Are you a whistle pig?" he asked playfully. The marmot whistled once more. "I guess you are. I wish I could whistle like that."

Clouds were forming quickly up and down the range as he reached the mountain. He could imagine what a

----

emerge from come out of
With spirits rising he bounded He felt good as he jumped
talus slopes tumbling bottom rocks coming out

lightning storm on the peak would be like; he wasted no time picking a route. There was only one by which he had a chance of reaching the summit, and that was the knife-edge in front of him where two planes of the Pyramid met. He left the pikas and the marmots behind and started picking his way up the knife-edge. Now it was all rock. Some of the rocks were loose and could **take him with them**. A fall down either **face** would be deadly, but the north side would be the worst. He'd slide a thousand feet on the snow before being **pitched** onto the boulders below.

Cloyd kept climbing and tried to keep his mind on each step, each handhold. The air was thin and **seared his lungs**. Every time he reached a spot that might have stopped him, he found a way around or located cracks and footholds that enabled him to continue. The clouds were building and starting to darken, but they were still in the distance. Cloyd felt strong. He remembered that first day at the old man's farm when he climbed to the outcrop, found the bearstone, and **fastened his longing on** these

....

take him with them make him fall
face side
pitched thrown
seared his lungs made it difficult to breathe
fastened his longing on decided that he wanted to climb

peaks. He fell into the rhythm of climbing and proceeded up the knife-edge at a steady, careful pace.

A calm joy lifted Cloyd up the final piece of the climb. He was as sure he'd make the top as he'd ever been of anything. He seemed to float up the last little bit and stepped to the very tip of the Pyramid.

Peaks on all sides were riding in the blue sky. Peaks everywhere, dancing, jutting up, **all in motion**. He had to sit down and grip the rock. Peaks, as far as he could see, peaks, rock and green tundra, snow banks, spruce forests, river canyons.

As he caught his breath, Cloyd saw a big bird soaring far below. Probably it was an eagle. He enjoyed its mastery of the winds, then watched it disappear. A storm was **gathering** in the Needles, and **shadows were overtaking the mountainsides**. Out in the low country, the sun was still shining. He was amazed to recognize the Chuska Mountains in the **hazy** distance. They were the same mountains he always saw from White Mesa. Home wasn't really so far away. Someday he'd go home, he knew, but it didn't have to be soon. Whenever it happened would

....

all in motion looking like they were moving

gathering coming soon

shadows were overtaking the mountainsides clouds were making everything dark

hazy foggy

be all right. Cloyd pulled the blue stone from his pocket and set the little bear on a flat rock at the very top of the mountain. "Lone Bear," he said aloud, "we're not so alone anymore."

Cloyd thought about how Walter liked to be deep in the cold darkness of his gold mine. He wished the old man could have stood here with him. He wanted to tell him *this* is the heart of the mountains, up here in the light where you can see forever. Where you feel like you're a part of it all, like the beating heart of the mountains is your own heart. He'd never felt this way before, free and peaceful at the same time. If only there was a way to show the old man how thankful he was, for this, for Blueboy, for everything. He could show he cared for Walter like a son for a father.

The wind began to blow hard, and **the temperature was dropping**. He'd have to start down soon. He wished he could stay longer and try to take it all in, but it didn't matter. He had **fulfilled his dream**. It would be something he could always **keep with him.**

Then he remembered what his grandmother had told him, how the Utes knew all these mountains. Other

----

the temperature was dropping it was getting cold
fulfilled his dream met his goal
keep with him remember

Utes like himself must have stood on this same peak years ago. They had probably done something special, said or sung something. Then Cloyd recalled a ceremony his grandmother had taught him, but which he'd never done. Taking the bearstone in his hand, he held it out and **offered it in turn** to the Four Directions, then to the Earth and the Sky.

....

offered it in turn presented it

BEFORE YOU MOVE ON...

1. **Setting** Reread page 162. Why did Cloyd think the top of the Pyramid was the "heart of the mountains"?

2. **Comparisons** How did Walter and Cloyd achieve their goals? How were the goals different?

LOOK AHEAD Read pages 164–168 to find out what Cloyd sees on the way back to camp.

Cloyd wants to tell Walter about his adventures, but he finds the bear hunter with Walter. Cloyd makes a big mistake.

17

Cloyd was eager now to be on his way back to the old man. But he wouldn't take the shortest way; there was more he wanted to see. Dropping through the deep timber, he picked up the Divide trail and followed it until he sighted Ute Lake, a deep green **crater** tucked under the north slope at timberline.

On the way down he saw three bull elk grazing in the lush grass along a **rivulet that fed** the lake. When they heard the horse coming down the **switchbacks**, the elk hurried up the far side of the basin and into the brushy mountain willows beyond.

At lakeside, Cloyd made his camp and hobbled his horses in the good grass. Before long he had his rod and reel assembled and was searching for bait. He found a tiny

....

crater large hole
rivulet that fed small stream that went into
switchbacks trails

grasshopper and dropped it on the surface of the deep and rocky lake, but the fish weren't interested. They could see its legs kicking, but they weren't interested. He tried the salmon eggs. **No luck.** The trout started hitting the surface for flies even tinier than gnats. He wondered if the old Utes had fished at this lake named after them, and how. He laughed out loud. He doubted they were **fly fishermen**.

As the sun was dropping behind the Needles, he sat by his fire and ate a chili supper. It tasted good, and the packhorse would have one less can to carry. **Warmth and contentment spread through his body.**

Cloyd's fourth morning found him riding out of Ute Lake up to the Divide and descending into the long alpine basin called the Rincon La Osa, which would lead him back to the valley of the Pine. This night he'd be at the mine with Walter, he thought happily. He thought about how he was going to tell the old man about that moment when his eyes and Blueboy's met, that he'd found out the answer to the question of whether horses could care about you. The red-haired man was wrong about horses, at least about this one. He had a lot he wanted to talk about with

....

No luck. The fish did not want them.

fly fisherman people who used fake flies to catch fish

Warmth and contentment spread through his body. He felt happy and warm.

Walter. He wondered if Walter would **recognize how much he'd grown** in four days' time.

He stopped to rest and eat berries on the bank of the Rincon stream as it wound its way slowly across a small meadow below the long basin. Kneeling by the stream to drink, he **marveled at the clarity** of the water, which seemed to magnify every pebble on the bottom. He became aware that he was looking as well at the dark backs of three large trout, motionless except for the fanning of their fins.

One of them, perhaps becoming aware of him, darted up a tiny inlet on his side of the creek. Cloyd followed and **kept his eye on** the fish moving slowly up the narrow passage. He'd like to catch this fish, he thought, catch it somehow without a fishing pole. Was it true what his grandmother had said, that in the old days some of the Utes could catch fish in their bare hands?

He would try. The fish would have to come back to the stream sometime. He could pick a spot and wait for it to come through.

With one knee on each **bank**, Cloyd straddled the

....

recognize how much he'd grown see that he had changed
marveled at the clarity was amazed by the clearness
kept his eye on watched
bank side of the stream

inlet. Slowly he lowered his hands and then his arms into the icy water as deep as his arms were long. And then he waited.

Five minutes, ten minutes, he couldn't tell anymore. His arms went numb, his back ached, but he **didn't move a muscle**. He could see the trout slowly swimming toward him, pausing here and there for long minutes.

The trout was close now. Cloyd could see its mouth working, its bright orange markings. It was looking through the tunnel his hands and arms made. Would it **retreat** or dart between his hands before he could close on it? He held them as still as he could. It swam still closer. He began to narrow the gap between his freezing hands, slowly, slowly, slowly. Unsuspecting, the cutthroat swam between them. Cloyd closed in as calmly as he could. He dug with his nails, grasped the fish, and lifted it in one motion out of the water and onto the bank.

He stood up to ease the striking pain in his back. The horses whinnied. A dark shape was moving at the edge of the meadow. An animal loping with **an unusual gait**. A bear! A huge brown bear, and it was aware of him. It stood on its hind legs to have a look at him, and its head swayed back and forth. Cloyd was astonished at how tall

....

didn't move a muscle did not move at all

retreat go back

an unusual gait a strange walk

it was. Its claws were enormous. The bear dropped quickly to all fours and suddenly disappeared into the trees.

The big fish flip-flopped against Cloyd's leg. He nudged it back into the water with his foot, then leaped across the Rincon stream and took off running in hopes of a second glimpse of the huge bear. Once in the trees Cloyd walked softly, looking all around, and tried to listen for the bear's **passage**. All he could hear was the furious pounding of his own heart.

In the quiet darkness of the trees, **the bear was nowhere and everywhere**. Suddenly Cloyd felt foolish and reckless for having tried to follow. He ran back to the sunlit meadow, to the horses. He wanted to hurry back to the camp on Snowslide Creek. He wanted to tell the old man about the bear.

....

passage footsteps

the bear was nowhere and everywhere the bear could be anywhere

BEFORE YOU MOVE ON...

1. **Comparisons** Reread pages 75 and 167–168. How was the bear that Cloyd saw different from the bear that Rusty killed at the ranch?

2. **Character** How did Cloyd feel about seeing Walter? What does this show about Cloyd?

LOOK AHEAD Cloyd is surprised when he gets to camp. Read pages 169–176 to see what happens.

It was late afternoon when he rode into camp. He was anxious to see Walter. The old man was drinking coffee and visiting by the campfire with his friend Rusty, the red-haired man.

Walter's face lit up when he saw Cloyd. "I didn't expect you until tomorrow or so," he said. "How'd everything go?"

"Fine," Cloyd mumbled. All his **enthusiasm was squelched**. The tall man was looking him over, like he did before. No handshake this time, but all the feelings were the same as before.

"Cloyd here's been out exploring the mountains. Did you climb that Rio Grande Pyramid?"

Cloyd nodded halfheartedly. He felt so disappointed that someone else was there, and worse, that it was the red-haired man. This wasn't how it was supposed to be.

"My goodness, that must've been something. I'll bet you could see hundreds of miles from up there."

"See any wildlife?" the outfitter asked **abruptly**.

Cloyd's heart began to pound. This wasn't as he'd pictured it, telling Walter how he'd caught the fish and seen the bear. But the outfitter had **brought the subject up**,

---

enthusiasm was squelched excitement ended
abruptly quickly
brought the subject up asked about wild animals

and the man was making him feel bad again, sick even, as if he was suddenly burning up with fever. He **cast** wildly about thinking for what to say or do, but he couldn't think; he could only feel the **resentment** burning inside, and he wanted to prove himself, show that he wasn't a nothing, show that he knew something, something that would impress the big hunter. He'd seen a bear without having had to **track it down** with dogs. "Some elk . . . " he said, **teetering on the brink**, and then he added, " . . . and a bear."

"When'd you see the bear?" the man asked quickly.

"Today."

"What kind?"

Cloyd hesitated. "He was brown. I guess he was a brown bear."

"**No such varmint.** Black bear in a cinnamon phase. How big?"

"Taller than you, standing up."

The red-haired man smiled condescendingly. "Me standing up, you say, or the bear?"

"Both."

....

cast looked

resentment hatred

track it down find it

teetering on the brink pausing

No such varmint. There are no animals like that here.

The man grunted. "You saw this bear standing on its hind legs? How far away was he?"

Now Cloyd regretted he'd said anything at all. Suddenly he didn't feel good about seeing the bear. The man was making him feel bad, making it seem in front of Walter like he was exaggerating. Maybe he was, a little, but he really didn't think so. What could he do now? He saw what he saw, and he wouldn't let the tall man shame him. "Just across the meadow," he said.

The man lifted his red eyebrows. "Oh, whereabouts?"

Again he hesitated. "Rincon," he said finally.

"Oh? La Vaca or La Osa?"

"La Osa."

"Rincon of the Bear, eh?" he said skeptically, with a wide grin. "Walter, you think he **might've let his imagination get away from him** up in that high altitude?"

Agitated, Walter got up. The conversation had gone badly. Cloyd had been embarrassed. His friend **had no feel for** the boy at all. "Why no, Rusty," he declared, "that ain't possible. **Cloyd's got an eye for detail better'n mine by far.**"

....

might've let his imagination get away from him only imagined that he saw the bear

had no feel for did not understand or care about

Cloyd's got an eye for detail better'n mine by far. Cloyd notices nature better than I do.

The tall man rose, hung his coffee cup in the branch of a tree, and crossed the fire circle to Cloyd. He clapped Cloyd's shoulder. "No hard feelings, kid. I believed every word you said. I'm just part lawyer, I guess, and curious **to boot**. Say, I've got to be going, Walter—my brothers are expecting me for supper."

Walter put together a meal for the boy. They ate quietly. Walter didn't pester him; he could see Cloyd didn't want to talk just now. Walter **let his mind drift, mulling things over**. Like about how he'd been single-jacking all this time the boy was gone, day and night practically, when he'd told the boy he wouldn't. He was nearly ready to fire and should be getting some sleep, lest he make a mistake during the **crucial** preparation of the charges.

Cloyd's grown, Walter reflected. He's stronger, more like a young man than a boy. Because of how it went with Rusty, he'd have to wait awhile before asking Cloyd about the ride. They should've shared the ride in the first place. On the other hand, sometimes it was better to be out there on your own. That's when you really see things and learn

....

to boot also
let his mind drift, mulling things over was thinking
crucial most important

something. Cloyd got to have the whole country to himself.

Tomorrow he'd fire the hole. Funny, it didn't really matter if he found anything. How could he expect to with only two blasts? That wasn't a significant amount of progress. But it was the trying again that made it worthwhile. This round might be his last ever. All his steels were dull, and it wouldn't do any good to try to sharpen them anymore—they needed **retempering**. The summer was run out anyway. His life, for that matter, was about run. But he'd come back to the Pride of the West the way he'd always wanted to, come **full circle**.

There was something **weighing in the air tonight**, Walter thought, something weighing on this time that should be savored. As he watched the boy in the firelight, he saw it building. Maybe Cloyd, too, was realizing that the summer was about over. It wouldn't do any good to talk about it. **There'd be time yet for ending on the upside.**

It was Cloyd who broke the long silence. "Why did he keep asking me about that bear I saw?"

....

retempering to be fixed

full circle back to the place where he had started

weighing in the air tonight that made tonight seem special

There'd be time yet for ending on the upside. There would still be time to end the summer in a good way.

"How do you mean?"

"He didn't believe me."

"Oh, he was trying to pick your memory."

Cloyd shook his head decisively. "He wanted to catch me saying something that wasn't right so he could prove I was **making it up**."

"Oh, no. I know Rusty awful well. He was so interested he could hardly hold himself still. Didn't you see how fast he took off? He was bustin' to get back to camp and get started after that bear. Sounded like a trophy."

Cloyd struggled against the panic that ripped him. His breath caught short, and his heart pounded in his ears. "It's not hunting season," he said, as calmly as he could. "Bear season was in June, wasn't it?"

"**Open season on bears, Cloyd, or there's hunts off and on** all year, I forget which."

Cloyd's mind raced. He'd **given away the bear**, and the outfitter was going to try to kill it. "Does he have those dogs with him?"

"They don't use any on this hunt. Too easy, they say. You see, Rusty and his brothers get together every summer

....

making it up lying; telling a story

Open season on bears, Cloyd, or there's hunts off and on You can hunt bears at any time, or there are special days when you can hunt

given away the bear told where the bear was

for a pleasure-hunt. It's kind of a contest. The first brother to get himself a bear wins a prize of some kind."

"They can find a bear without dogs?"

"They're awful good. Rusty's the best trapper, tracker, and hunter in the San Juans. As a matter of fact, they're bowhunting."

"What do you mean?"

"Why, with bows and arrows. That's the way Rusty favors. He even writes articles for a magazine about bowhunting."

"There was a rifle in the case on his horse."

"Well, he'd have it along with him. But he prefers to bowhunt because it takes quite a bit more skill. It's like the Indians used to, only the arrows are made out of fiberglass or some-such and the head's like three razor blades in one. You wouldn't want to touch the thing—it'd take your thumb off. Even so, **the odds against the hunter getting close enough are pretty long**. Sometimes these guys **come up empty-handed**. Take this hunt for instance. They'll be heading back sometime soon and **still have nothing to show**. They probably won't come within miles of that bear of yours. Bears cover a lot of ground, you know.

....

the odds against the hunter getting close enough are pretty long most hunters do not get close enough to the bear

come up empty-handed do not kill any bears

still have nothing to show not have a bear with them

The chances of finding any one bear with that kind of head start are slim at best."

Cloyd wasn't reassured. The old man said the outfitter was the best trapper, tracker, and hunter in the mountains. This man might very well kill the bear, and he'd told him where to find it. Now he'd done it, spoiled everything. In the old days, his grandmother said, the Utes wouldn't kill bears. That would bring on the worst of bad luck, she said. Cloyd considered his secret name and fingered the bearstone in his pocket. He had to **undo** his mistake.

....

undo fix

BEFORE YOU MOVE ON...

1. **Conflict** Cloyd hated Rusty, but he told him about the grizzly. Why did he do this?

2. **Character's Motive** Why did Cloyd need to "undo his mistake"?

LOOK AHEAD Read pages 177–183 to find out what happens when Cloyd tries to stop Rusty.

Cloyd tries to stop the hunter. At the same time,
Walter goes back into the mine to blast alone.

18

Cloyd hoped to slip out of camp as soon as the moon rose to light his way. He struggled to stay awake after Walter fell asleep, but soon failed, worn out by his long ride off the Divide. The moon was high in the sky when he awoke. He feared that the red-haired man had already gone up the Rincon **after** the bear. The old man's breathing whistled its usual song; Cloyd was able to collect his jacket and slide through the tent flap without waking him.

He climbed in the moonlight to a **vantage point** above the **confluence** of the Rincon creek and the Pine River, and waited, **his confidence collapsing all around him**. He was alarmed by every sound the night made.

To his relief, he finally spotted the outfitter riding up the Pine trail. It was still all but dark, yet Cloyd

....

after to look for
vantage point place where he might see the hunter
confluence meeting place
his confidence collapsing all around him feeling afraid

recognized the profile of the tall man. He wondered why the man was alone, then recalled the contest among the brothers. The outfitter **wanted the bear all for himself.**

In the first light the outfitter trotted his horse along the flats at the bottom of the Rincon creek. From the point the man disappeared into the trees, the trail climbed so abruptly that his horse would be slowed to a walk. Cloyd ran to **keep up**. He wished he had Blueboy, but a horse would **give him away** turning over stones and breaking sticks. He had to follow so carefully that the best tracker in the mountains wouldn't know he was being followed.

Maybe the bear's gone over the mountains, Cloyd hoped, across the rockslides where even the red-haired man couldn't track him. But what if he had just killed a deer and would stay in the Rincon to feed a few days? What if he's eating berries along the stream in the meadow?

Cloyd hurried up the mountain, cutting the switchbacks and watching to make sure he didn't come too close to the man on horseback. Finally he could see through the trees to the meadow, the one where he'd seen

....

wanted the bear all for himself did not want anyone else to have the bear

keep up get closer to the hunter

give him away make too much noise

the bear. He stopped to take off his jacket. **He'd soaked himself** with sweat. The outfitter, he guessed, was even now on the meadow looking for signs. Cloyd crawled to the edge of the trees and peeked around the trunk of a large spruce.

He saw the horse first, then the man kneeling in the grass where the bear had loped toward the trees and stood up. It hadn't taken the tall man much time to find the track of the bear. He was as skillful as Walter said, and after all, Cloyd thought bitterly, he'd been told right where to go.

As eager as he might be, the red-haired man took his time examining the signs, especially around the place where the bear stood up. Then he climbed **the tongue of a talus slide to a spot well** above the meadow where he crouched awhile and scanned in all directions with his large binoculars.

In a bowl like this any sound would carry, Cloyd knew, yet the outfitter descended the slope as quietly as a cat. He's hunting, Cloyd realized—he's deadly serious. Cloyd remembered how the red-haired man had

....

He'd soaked himself His body was wet

the tongue of talus slide to a spot well an area of loose rock to a place far

In a bowl like this any sound would carry In this valley, footsteps and other noises would echo

almost laughed at him. If the man knew, he would simply **sneer at the suggestion** that an unarmed boy on foot hoped to stop him.

How could it be done? Maybe make enough noise to warn the bear? That's what he'd been thinking as he rushed up the trail. But if he yelled and scared the bear away, wouldn't the man catch up again? How could the bear escape the best tracker in the country?

Cloyd watched the man return to the signs on the meadow. Most likely he hadn't caught sight of the bear through the binoculars.

The outfitter packed a daypack with his binoculars and what must have been food and water. Cloyd watched him string his bow and check his arrows one by one. How close would you have to get, Cloyd wondered, to hunt with a bow and arrow? The man hobbled his horse, entered the trees where the bear had, and disappeared.

The man's rifle must be in the saddle **scabbard** on the horse, Cloyd reasoned. With the rifle he could make plenty of noise. The mountains would echo the shots all the way to the bear, wherever it was.

The rifle was there in the scabbard, as he'd hoped.

....

sneer at the suggestion laugh if anyone told him
scabbard sheath

But when Cloyd pulled the bolt back and **exposed the chamber**, there was no ammunition in it. He searched the saddlebags—no shells! The outfitter must have them in his daypack. The man was gone now, the chance to keep him in sight lost.

Cloyd knew he lacked the skill to track the man or the bear in the woods. His only chance now was to get back to the trees on the other side of the meadow, **on the slope opposite the one the man was on**. That way he could climb without being seen and find a high place where he might spot the outfitter again—if he was lucky.

Cloyd worked for most of an hour until he found a lookout close to timberline, high above the **dogleg** between the lower and upper meadows. **Great ups and downs rippled** the upper basin, where even now the outfitter or the bear or both might be hidden from view. Big patches of stunted spruce dotted the flanks of the basin, and thickets of brush grew everywhere, looking from this distance like tall grass. A thousand places he couldn't see. I'm an unlucky person, he thought.

....

exposed the chamber looked inside

on the slope opposite the one the man was on on the hill across from the man

dogleg bend in the trail

Great ups and downs rippled There were many hills near

Cloyd can't be too **far off**, Walter thought. He didn't take the horse. He'll be back. Walter's mind drifted back to his work, as he readied the charges for the second blast. Once you blast, he reflected, you forget about all the backbreaking work. Another three or four feet of the mountain is broken loose, and you just never know what you're going to find. Most times nothing but rock. **A bonanza, he mused, is a hole in the ground owned by a champion liar.** But sometimes a man found good ore, and once in a million lifetimes, a fabulous strike like the Cresson Vug. It's really gambling, is what it is, he thought. They ought to make it illegal.

Walter came running out of the tunnel hollering, "Fire in the hole! Fire in the hole!" even though there was no one to hear it but himself. Muffled somewhat, the blast sent fewer clouds of fumes and dust than usual out of the mouth of the mine. He was concerned that the explosion **lacked punch**. When the air cleared enough for him to see, he entered the mine. So what if the air's still bad, he thought. No sense in an old man babying his lungs.

He groaned when he saw the blasted face at the end of the tunnel, recognizing at once what was wrong. The

....

far off far away

A bonanza, he mused, is a hole in the ground owned by a champion liar. There are no mines full of gold.

lacked punch wasn't powerful enough

old face had been only partially blown out; two mounds of rock **held the bulk of it fast. Two missed shots**—worse than rotten luck. Two mounds of rock clinging there with crucial charges inside, unshot but possibly hair-triggered to blow when a man tried to pick at the surrounding rock to get at them.

Outside, he sat and thought about the missed shots. He could wait until next summer to try to pick them out, but then **they'd be hanging over his head** all winter and he'd still have to face them. He could give up on the Pride of the West, he supposed. But one thing he couldn't do— wait until somebody was blown up fooling around inside the mine. If he was going to remove them, he'd better try while he had the nerve and while the boy was safely away **blowing off steam**. "Maude, you were right—it's a risky business," he said aloud.

He lit the headlamp, shouldered the pick, and entered the tunnel. More than anything, he had to know if the missed shots hid some decent ore.

....

held the bulk of it fast were not blown away

Two missed shots Two sticks of dynamite did not explode

they'd be hanging over his head he would worry about them

blowing off steam feeling angry about something

BEFORE YOU MOVE ON...

1. **Summarize** Why was it difficult for Cloyd to stop Rusty? Give three reasons.

2. **Cause and Effect** Reread page 183. Why was it dangerous for Walter to look for the missed shots?

LOOK AHEAD Read pages 184–193 to find out what happens to the bear.

Cloyd cannot stop Rusty from killing the grizzly.
But Cloyd might have a way to punish the hunter
for harming the bear.

19

The hours of careful waiting and watching ended as the tall white clouds turned dark and the wind began to blow. Cloyd glimpsed a figure moving swiftly for a low spot several miles up the basin. If it was the man **on the track of the bear**, it meant the bear had moved up the Rincon in the direction of the Divide.

Cloyd took off running. He avoided the meadows and tried to **make time in** the stands of timber and in the brush. He glimpsed the figure again clearing the top of the Divide, vanishing just as lightning struck up there. Apparently the outfitter had dropped his tracking and hurried up the ridge while Cloyd was in the brush. The man was taking a risk climbing into the weather, Cloyd

....

on the track of the bear following the bear's path
make time in move quickly through

thought. He must be **closing in on** the bear.

Cloyd **broke into the open and made for** the place where the man went over the top. As he climbed, it began to **sprinkle**; he had no rain gear. He ran stumbling up the ridge and into the wind with no thought but that he had to reach the bear in time.

As he topped out on the Divide, he found the outfitter's straw cowboy hat weighted and left in plain sight—as a sign for his brothers? Cloyd thought the man must be a little farther east on the Divide and a little below it. He had to be, it was the only hidden place. If he'd gone on down the steep slope to the west, he'd be visible.

The thundershower had passed by and was attacking the Pyramid. The day was waning now; he knew he had to guess right.

Yes, the outfitter had to be tucked out of sight on one of the small terraces angling to the north and dropping like stairs down to Ute Lake. The man—and the bear— must be about where he'd passed the day before on his way up from the lake.

....

closing in on getting closer to

broke into the open and made for stopped hiding and tried to get to

sprinkle rain a little

Just in case the outfitter had somehow doubled back, Cloyd checked behind. His eye caught a flash of bright yellow. Riders in rainslickers, three of them coming up the Rincon and leading a fourth horse. The brothers. He left the ridgeline quickly.

Cloyd found the highest terrace, but the man wasn't there. He ran its length, then crawled to the far edge to avoid being seen as he **gained a vantage point**. Below him lay another little meadow surrounded by rockslides and brush. He made his way down to it among the rocks and ran for the far end. The wind blowing hard against him slowed him down.

When he dropped at the far end of the meadow to look below, he saw them on the next shelf. It *was* the biggest bear he'd seen, a huge brown bear turning over rocks above the mountain willows at the edge of the meadow, looking maybe for pikas or marmots. The outfitter was **stalking in a crouch**. He sneaked along the line of brush until he drew close to the bear on the other side. The man carried his bow with an arrow in place. The bear wasn't aware of him.

....

Just in case the outfitter had somehow doubled back, Cloyd checked behind. Cloyd looked behind him to see if the hunter had come back.

gained a vantage point found a place to see

stalking in a crouch crawling toward the bear

Cloyd yelled **with all his might**. Strangely, neither the bear nor the man paid any attention. The red-haired man drew close to a gap in the brushline. Cloyd screamed again and again, desperately, with no result. As close as they were, the bear and the man were deaf and unreachable, like **phantoms** in a dream. Then he realized that he was yelling from above and into a sturdy wind, and his voice was being blown away, up and behind him.

Suddenly the tall man stood out in the open in front of the bear with the bow pulled all the way back and the arrow aimed. Sensing something, the bear stood up as if to have a better look and **took the arrow in its neck**.

The bear didn't fall. It roared in pain and **charged** the man through the opening in the brush with **uncanny** speed. But the outfitter hadn't wasted any time nocking a second arrow, and released it into the bear's chest.

Still the bear came on, all teeth and claws and blood, and knocked aside the bow the man lifted to shield himself. As the man spun away, the big bear hesitated, then stood up and tried to brush away the arrowshafts with its paws.

....

with all his might very loudly

phantoms ghosts

took the arrow in its neck the arrow hit the bear in the neck

charged ran to attack

uncanny incredible

The man crouched and **brandished** a long-bladed knife. Returning to all fours, the bear took a few steps toward him, gave a strangled growl, and **collapsed** on its side.

The red-haired man circled the fallen bear several times. Then he knelt and ran his hand across its broad forehead. He inspected the teeth and the underside of one of the front paws, and sized the claws against his forefinger.

Cloyd fell to his belly in the cover of the rocks and let the bitterness roll over him in waves. He dreaded being seen by the outfitter now—that would make **the man's victory complete**. He'd gladly sink into the ground if he could. The uncaring wind shifted and carried the fragment of a shout from above and behind him. The others were coming, the brothers. He had to get out of there. He **scuttled** backward until he was well away from the lip of the shelf, then stood and ran off the downhill side into the rocks on the steep slope below. Above him, the riders crossed the spot he'd fled.

There was whooping and shouting as the three men

....

brandished pulled out
collapsed fell down
the man's victory complete Rusty feel even happier
scuttled moved

met up with their brother and the dead bear, but Cloyd couldn't see them and he couldn't hear the outfitter's voice. He had to hear what the man would say. He worked his way through the talus until he was directly below them, then crept under the edge of the meadow where he could hear.

"Biggest bear I ever saw," said one. "You win again."

"You sure **got the jump on us**, Rusty, sneaking off in the night like that," said a second brother. "We came as soon as we saw your note. Helluva bear. Did he charge you? How'd it go?"

"Look at the forehead," the outfitter said, not so loud as the others.

"What about it?"

"It's dished out."

"So?"

"Look at the hump on its back, the forehead, the teeth, the claws—that's a grizzly."

"Everybody knows there aren't any grizzlies left in Colorado," the third brother protested.

"Wasn't true. This here's a grizzly."

"If you say so—you're the expert. Well then, you've sure got yourself a trophy here, Rusty."

....

got the jump on us were faster than us

"What I've got myself here is a **heck of a mess**."

"**Waddaya** mean?"

"It's illegal to kill a grizzly. They're protected. Hundred thousand dollar fine and a year in jail."

"So . . . you didn't know it was a grizzly, did you?"

"It . . . crossed my mind—I couldn't tell for sure until I was up close. . . . it charged me—**I had to defend myself.**"

That's a lie, Cloyd thought. That's not how it happened.

"Well, who's to know?" one of the brothers snapped. "Ain't nobody's business but yours."

"I got carried away."

There was a pause, then Cloyd heard the red-haired man's voice fill with what almost seemed like regret. "It's probably one of the two cubs that were reported around the Pyramid ten or twelve years ago."

"Look, Rusty," the same brother said, "Quit worrying. You made a terrific kill here, and it'll make a once-in-a-lifetime trophy."

"You guys think I can go ahead and display it in my

....

heck of a mess problem

Waddaya What do you

I had to defend myself. I killed it to protect myself.

"I got carried away." "I did not think about what I was doing."

home—show it to the game warden when he comes over to visit?"

"I **see your point**. You've got a problem here, don't you? How 'bout I just take it back to Texas with me. Let's **skin it out** right now."

"I don't know, Andy. I could lose my license over this—that's my **livelihood** we're talking about. Even if a grizzly's found dead, you're supposed to report it as soon as you can so the Department of Wildlife's scientific guys can study it."

"C'mon, we'll pack the skin out good and careful. No one'll ever see it. Tell you what. I'll give you a thousand dollars for it, make it worth your while. I'd really like to have that monster **baring** his teeth on the floor in front of the fireplace. Look at the size of those claws! From what you're saying, if you do report this thing, there's no way they aren't going to take it away from you. Then what if they don't like your story? You'll end up without the bear and in big trouble both!"

"We'd have to leave the **carcass**, Andy. Backpackers

....

see your point understand
skin it out take off its skin
livelihood job
baring showing
carcass body

would come across it and report it. The bone structure would identify it as a grizzly. Sam Perkins—the game warden—he knows we're up here. **I'd never get away with it.** Besides, he's a good friend. The more I think about this, the more I'm convinced that the only way I'm going to come out at all on this deal is to **get ahold of** Sam right away. He's going to want to bring in the department helicopter and lift this grizzly out as soon as possible, before it starts to spoil. So let's get down to the guard station and radio this in."

"It's a helluva shame."

"Sure is," the outfitter agreed. "But I'm not going to risk my business over it."

After the men were gone, Cloyd approached the bear. Kneeling close to its massive head, Cloyd **asked the bear's forgiveness.** He prayed that somehow this bear wasn't the last one. Hadn't there been two cubs? Maybe there are others that nobody knows about. **Overcome with grief**, he stared into darkness. Cloyd vowed to the mighty grizzly that he would remember him forever, not lifeless like now,

....

I'd never get away with it. He would find out what I did.
get ahold of find
asked the bear's forgiveness told the bear he was sorry
Overcome with grief Feeling sad and guilty

but standing tall and alert, sniffing the wind, still the most powerful animal in the mountains.

As he fled down the Rincon trail, the night was full of accusing voices. A large owl suddenly flapped out of the dark and almost struck him. He yelled sharply in terror. His grandmother had told him about owls. This one would be the dead bear's spirit **freshly loosed** from its body.

....

freshly loosed free

BEFORE YOU MOVE ON...

1. **Summarize** Tell what Cloyd saw from the mountain.

2. **Character's Point of View** How did Rusty feel about killing the grizzly?

LOOK AHEAD Read pages 194–202 to find out what decisions Cloyd makes next.

Cloyd finds Walter in the mine. The old rancher is badly hurt. Cloyd desperately searches for help. Can he save Walter?

20

It was no accident he'd seen the owl, Cloyd discovered. When, in the middle of the night, he stumbled into camp and lifted the flap of the canvas tent, **his misgivings were verified**. Instead of the musical **comings and goings** of the old man's breath, he was greeted by an uncanny silence. He had to fumble for a flashlight. Indeed, Walter was not there. His sleeping bag was rolled up as it always was during the day. The old man had not been to bed this night at all.

Cloyd ran up the ore dump and into the mine. His flashlight caught the trace of dust lingering in the air. There'd been a blast, he knew. **And with that knowledge came the sickening realization** that Walter had been

....

his misgivings were verified he knew that something was wrong

comings and goings sound

And with that knowledge came the sickening realization And Cloyd knew

194

working all along and had **set off another round of blasting**. He listened. All he could hear was the beating of his own heart. If Walter was working in there, he should be able to hear it: any sound carried in the mine. But there was no sound at all coming down the tunnel, only the uncanny silence. He called. No answer.

Cloyd found him face down at the end of the tunnel. Only the old man's head, shoulders, and right arm showed above the rubble. The explosion had **made meat of** one side of his face. Cloyd knelt close. Walter was still breathing, but he was unconscious. There was a nasty gash in his scalp on the back of his head, and it was all matted with blood. Cloyd went to work to free the old man from the rubble. He worked with the flashlight in his teeth, so he could use both hands. It took time. He **fought the panic that was making his head swim**. He had to be able to think. What was he going to do? How much time did the old man have? The legs were pinned badly, but at last he freed them, and then he saw the fracture. Surrounded by blood and dirt, the broken bone of the old man's lower leg was sticking out, and it had a sharp point on it.

....

set off another round of blasting blasted dynamite in the mine again

made meat of almost destroyed

fought the panic that was making his head swim tried to be brave

Cloyd felt dizzy, he felt the panic rising again, and he fought it. He had to get Walter outside. He picked him up as gently as he could and started out of the mine. He didn't know if he'd be strong enough to make it, but he clenched his teeth, straightened his back, and kept moving. Cloyd let the flashlight drop from his fingers as he reached the portal; outside there was moonlight and even the first hint of dawn. Then **it came to him**, his only chance to get help fast. A helicopter. *A helicopter was coming to get the bear.* He stumbled and then recovered. It felt like he was carrying three hundred pounds. He told himself how light the old man was, and he kept going until he reached the tent.

Cloyd laid Walter down on a sleeping bag, then opened the other bag and spread it across him as a blanket. He knew he had to keep the old man warm. Then he ran down to the creek, drank from it, and splashed his face with the cold water. He had to think, and think right. Rusty said he was going to **radio for a helicopter** from the guard station. Where was that? He hadn't said—no clues at all. It could be any direction from where he killed the bear. How long would it have taken him to get there?

....

it came to him he had an idea
radio for a helicopter call for a helicopter to come

There was no telling. How long before the helicopter came?

Dawn was coming on fast. Rusty probably reached the radio sometime in the evening. The helicopter could be coming anytime now; there was already enough daylight for them to fly. He could take Blueboy and head for the bear and hope to make it in time, but if he didn't—maybe he should ride all the way down the Pine to the trailhead and hitch to a phone and call for a helicopter. He had to choose, and it had to be the right decision. He went back to the old man. Walter was hurt so bad, and he was so fragile. There wasn't time enough to ride all the way down the Pine River, Cloyd decided. There just wasn't enough time.

He left drinking water by the old man's shoulder, in case he **came to**, and then he saddled the roan. Cloyd walked him to the creek, where he took a long drink, and then a second. "Now we're gonna ride, Blueboy, we're gonna run. I want you to run like you've never run before."

He mounted the horse and took off flying. They galloped down Snowslide Creek and then up the Pine,

....

There was no telling. There was no way to know.
Dawn was coming on fast. The sun was rising.
came to woke up

until they were slowed by the steep Rincon trail. Was there time? Was he doing the right thing?

The roan was climbing, climbing. His gray coat was soaked with sweat, and in the morning light it shone a royal blue. He drank from the Rincon stream when they reached the meadow, and then he **broke into a canter** when the trail leveled out in the long upper basin. "**Atta** Blue," Cloyd encouraged him. "Atta Blueboy. Do it for me."

The climb out of the Rincon slowed them to a walk again, and it seemed to take forever. The sun was climbing fast. Noon wasn't that far off. When they were still in the thick mountain willows, he heard the chop-chop-chop of a helicopter and then looked up and saw it for a moment. He waved frantically, but he knew there was no way it could have seen him. At least the copter is heading toward the bear, he thought. It couldn't be **on its way out**.

The last pitch up the Divide was steep and slow, and the precious minutes were flying by. Finally they topped out. The roan's mouth was all covered with foam, and **his sides were heaving**. Cloyd urged his horse down the other

....

broke into a canter ran faster

Atta Good job

on its way out already leaving

his sides were heaving he was breathing hard

side. "Run, Blue—**it's going to take off**! We're not going to **make it**!"

They came charging off the Divide. The helicopter came in sight, with its whirring blades and the awful noise and commotion they stirred. It was still on the ground. Cloyd couldn't see the bear—it was already loaded. Four men were walking back toward their horses and holding onto their hats. The roan pitched up to a stop and wouldn't budge, not with the chopping and the scent of the bear all around. Cloyd leaped off and ran down the mountainside, and then the men saw him coming. He ran straight for the red-haired man and screamed in his ear. Rusty turned and sprinted, dived low under the whirling blades, and hollered for the pilot to shut the helicopter down.

Six men crowded around him. He told them about the old man, told them to hurry. One of the brothers said, "Hey, how'd you know about this helicopter? How'd you know to come up here?" The red-haired man was watching him closely, and so was the game warden. Cloyd didn't answer. He yelled at them, pleaded for them to

....

it's going to take off the helicopter will leave
make it get there before it leaves

hurry. They dragged the bear out of the helicopter. It was enormous.

"You get in with me," the man in uniform said. "You and me and the pilot. Rusty'll take care of your horse."

"Tell Walter," said the outfitter, "tell him I'll bring all of his horses and his stuff out. Tell him not to worry about a thing."

Cloyd looked up and saw the red-haired man's eyes. **They were full of concern for his friend**; they were even kind for once. The man leaned forward and said, "You **done good**, boy. However you done it, you done awful good."

Cloyd looked away. He saw the bear all in a heap, with its teeth showing and the tongue caught between them. Flies were buzzing all around, walking in its mouth and on its eyes.

"Let's get moving!" the game warden yelled. He **gave Cloyd a push and a boost**, then climbed in himself, using the bear for a step.

....

They were full of concern for his friend Rusty's eyes showed how worried he was about Walter

done good did a good thing

gave Cloyd a push and a boost helped Cloyd get into the helicopter

200

The copter started up, and then they lifted off. The men and the bear shrank below, and Cloyd caught sight of Blueboy on the mountain. Then they cleared the Divide and headed down the Rincon toward the old man. "So how did you know that helicopter would be coming?" the game warden asked him. "Do you know something about that bear?"

Cloyd knew what Rusty would have told the game warden. Something like what he told his brothers. That the bear had charged, and he had to defend himself. He thought about how it really happened. How the bear stood up to sniff the wind, and took the arrow through its neck. He knew this was his chance to **get back at the red-haired man, to really show him**. His chance to get revenge.

And then Cloyd remembered the peach trees, and his awful revenge with the chain saw. He didn't want any more of that poison. He wouldn't say a thing. **What was done was done.** Rusty would **figure out** he'd been right there when it happened—that was enough.

....

get back at the red-haired man, to really show him get revenge on Rusty, to really prove him wrong

What was done was done. The bear was dead, and nothing could change that.

figure out know

The game warden was waiting for his answer. Cloyd shrugged and looked away, in so final a way that the man could tell he was going to have to wait forever. You might as well wait for a rock to speak.

BEFORE YOU MOVE ON...

1. **Cause and Effect** Why did the helicopter come to the mountain? How did this help Walter?

2. **Character's Motive** Reread pages 200–201. Why did Cloyd keep Rusty's secret?

LOOK AHEAD Read pages 203–213 to find out what difficult choice Cloyd has to make.

Cloyd visits Walter in the hospital. Walter cannot stay on the farm alone. Cloyd thinks of how he can help his friend.

21

Cloyd wasn't allowed in to see the old man. He came to the hospital every day and waited, but they wouldn't let him in yet. He took the bearstone out of his pocket and asked the nurse to put it by Walter. She said she would put it right on his nightstand where he would see it. Walter's brother was there, from his ranch down at Aztec, and so was his sister-in-law from Missouri. They got to see him first. Finally Cloyd was allowed in. Half of Walter's face was bandaged, and his leg was in a cast that was held off the bed a little with a pulley. He smiled painfully when he saw Cloyd and beckoned him over. "I'm gonna **make it**, Cloyd," he said. **"They can't kill this old hoss."**

Cloyd didn't say anything. He didn't know what to say. He just stood by the old man. Walter rolled his eyes

....

make it live

"They can't kill this old hoss." "I am not going to die yet."

toward the nightstand. "I sure appreciated seeing that blue bear of yours."

Cloyd looked at the bearstone in a new way. He'd been wishing, ever since he'd been to the top of the mountain, that he could find a way to show the old man how he felt about him. Now Cloyd knew what to do. He would give the old man **his greatest treasure**. "I want you to have it," Cloyd said, pointing to the bearstone with a twist of his lips.

The old man tried to hitch himself up in his bed. "Now wait a minute here, that's—"

Cloyd's eyes met Walter's. He wanted the old man to understand how grateful he was. "I want you to keep it," he said.

Walter saw into Cloyd's dark eyes and felt the strength and conviction of a man, not a boy. **He was greatly humbled to receive such a token of affection.** And at his age. This was a particular sort of joy he'd never felt in his whole life. He reached over to the nightstand and took the turquoise bear in his fingers. "I'll always treasure this piece, I surely will."

---

his greatest treasure the thing he loved the most

He was greatly humbled to receive such a token of affection. The gift made him feel very special.

A tear escaped the old man's eye. "I'll think of you every time I see it." For a while Walter couldn't speak. "Now then," he said finally, "you and me have a lot of **catchin' up** to do. I heard about what you did, how you rode that blue horse up the Divide and got me that helicopter. Nobody else could've done as much, Cloyd."

With a quick smile, Cloyd said, "You would've done the same for me."

And then it was time to go. Walter could only have short visits. It was September, and school was starting. Cloyd came after school to see the old man and talk for a little while, and then the nurses let him come early in the morning as well. Walter was going to be in the hospital a long time. Cloyd could see he really needed **company**. He told Walter about how school was much better than before, how he was going to learn how to read. His housemother got the school to give him a teacher all to himself for one period a day, since he was going to try.

A few weeks passed, and the old man seemed to be getting worse instead of better. Cloyd didn't know why.

....

catchin' up talking
company visitors

He was there when Walter's sister-in-law was saying good-bye, and then he found out something the old man had known for a while, but hadn't told him. "**You won't mind it so bad**, Walter," she said kindly. "You **just can't manage on your own**. If I could come and live at the farm, that would be another thing, but you know I have my own family back home. . . . "

"I wouldn't ask you to, Etta," Walter said.

"Well, I know you wouldn't have that. And Tom has his own ranch to **keep up with**. . . ."

The old man looked away through the window at the yellow leaves blowing from the trees, and he sighed.

His sister-in-law took his hand. "It's time to come in from the farm, Walter. Lots of folks have to **face that**. The nursing home's not going to be so bad, really, Walter. And I'll know you're getting good care."

The old man reached with his other hand and held fast. "I miss the farm awful bad, Etta. I could get my strength back on the farm."

"The doctor said it's going to be a long, slow process,

You won't mind it so bad It will not be too bad
just can't manage on your own cannot live alone
keep up with take care of
face that do the same thing

Walter. You can't afford a live-in nurse. **These bills have drawn you down too bad.** Now, we already talked about all that, Walter."

And then she said good-bye. She had to catch a plane back to Missouri. Cloyd sat awhile with the old man. "What's going to happen to the farm?" he asked.

"Have to sell it to pay **my board** at the nursing home. But now, let's **change the subject.** Tell me what you did today. . . . "

The reading teacher was talking, and Cloyd wasn't even listening to her. He was thinking about Walter, about how he was getting worse instead of better. Pretty soon they would move him out of the hospital, and then he would **wither away.** It wouldn't take long. If he couldn't get back to his farm, he was going to wither away.

"Cloyd, I thought you wanted to work with me," the teacher said.

"I'm sorry. I was thinking."

It came to him in the group home, when all the kids were watching television, and he was looking at it

....

These bills have drawn you down too bad. You have spent most of your money on hospital bills.

my board for a room

change the subject talk about something else

wither away become sicker and die

but not seeing anything. The next day, in front of the school, Cloyd asked around among the bus drivers and found the one who came in from the east, a burly man in grease-stained overalls. "Does your bus come in from the Piedra?" he asked the driver.

The man shook his head. "Not nearly. Starts this side of Bayfield."

The boy's disappointment showed. "How come you're askin'?" the driver asked.

"I need to come in to school from there."

"Oh? Whereabouts?"

"A farm north of the highway."

"Ain't that the Landis place?"

"You know him?"

"I live **out that way**. You must be the kid helped out with him in the summer. Hey, I heard about you. Name's Wilson," he said, **extending his grimy hand**. "Wilson Webb. 'Scuse the grease—I work at a garage in between drivin' the bus. You see, I drive my pickup over to Bayfield and park it where the bus run starts. I'd be happy to bring you in from the Piedra if that's what you're askin'—

....

"Ain't that the Landis place?" "Is that where Walter Landis lives?"

out that way near his house

extending his grimy hand putting out his dirty hand

wouldn't mind the company a bit."

Cloyd hurried back to the group home to tell his housemother. She wasn't there. He went to his room. A boy he'd never met before was unpacking a duffel bag and hanging up his clothes in Cloyd's closet. An army cot was set up between the beds. After a long moment of surprise, Cloyd asked him what was going on.

The boy shrugged. "Heard somebody was moving out. You, I guess."

"I didn't hear anything about it."

Cloyd **fretted** awhile in the living room, then saw Susan James driving up in the van and hurried out to see her. He stood quietly on the lawn and tried to **read her face** as she walked up. She knew something important.

"**Have I got some news for you**, Cloyd," she said excitedly.

Cloyd held his breath. He was always afraid of things dropped on him like this.

"The tribe says you can come home now, Cloyd."

"Home," he mumbled.

"White Mesa! They called this morning, Cloyd, and

....

fretted worried

read her face guess what she was thinking

Have I got some news for you I have something good to tell you

said everything looks a whole lot better at home, so—"

"How do you mean?" he asked guardedly.

"Well, the tribe heard about how hard you've been trying. They want to give you another chance at going to school right there in Blanding. Your grandmother's new job is working out, and your sister's on her way back from Salt Lake. Maybe your grandmother will get her goats back. Everybody's ready for you to come home, Cloyd."

He didn't know what to say. It was everything he'd hoped for all winter. "When?" he asked **blankly**.

"Right away! Well, tomorrow morning. Did you meet Charlie—in your room?"

Cloyd nodded.

"Sorry about that. When the people down at Towaoc heard **about the vacancy**, they sent Charlie up even though they were supposed to wait until tomorrow. But you know, there's a waiting list, and they've been desperately trying to find a place for him. . . . Why don't we go over to the hospital so you can say good-bye to Walter?"

Say good-bye to Walter? How could he do that, he asked himself, when the old man was slipping downhill? If he **deserted Walter** now . . . As much as he wanted to

....

blankly without emotion
about the vacancy that you were leaving
deserted Walter left Walter alone

go back to White Mesa, it wouldn't be right. **It was his turn to pay back some of what he'd been given.** "I can't go now," he told her. "Maybe after the winter . . ."

"Why not?"

"Walter needs me. He can't go back to the farm unless someone's there to do the chores and take care of—"

"But it's all arranged for him to go to the nursing home as soon as he—"

"He'll die there," Cloyd declared. "He's starting to die now."

She knew as much from visiting Walter herself. She'd been worrying terribly for him, knowing how badly he missed his farm. He'd been there so long he was like an old tree too deeply rooted for transplanting. "Tell me **how it would all work**, Cloyd. I guess you've got it all figured out."

Cloyd told her about the bus driver. He told her she'd have to get permission from the tribe for him to leave the group home and live with Walter.

"And permission from two school districts," she added. "You'd be out of boundaries. I don't know, Cloyd—it all sounds pretty tricky to me. I don't have any

---

It was his turn to pay back some of what he'd been given. Walter had helped him, and now he wanted to help Walter.

how it would all work about your idea

idea if the tribe would ever allow something like that. But then again, they might be able to see what kind of sacrifice you'd be making and why. Are you really sure about it yourself?"

Before he could answer, she told him, "Take a long walk and really think it over. Here's your chance to go home, Cloyd. Then come back and let me know what you've decided. If you want to stay with Walter until he's better, **I'll do my best to make it happen**."

Cloyd walked down to the river to think, crouched on the bank, and **turned it all over in his mind**. He saw himself standing at the door to a hospital room, discovering the shell of his father hooked up to a machine, and realizing finally that he didn't have a father. He saw himself finding the bearstone and killing the peach trees and following the old man up the Pine River to the mine. He saw himself standing alone atop the Rio Grande Pyramid and realizing **a father had come into his life** after all. He remembered the look in Blueboy's eye right before he tumbled down the mountain, and he recalled

....

I'll do my best to make it happen I will help you as much as I can

turned it all over in his mind thought about everything that had happened

a father had come into his life he had found someone who he loved like a father

the bear. He'd never forget the bear. . . . *The hurt you get over makes you stronger.* **It was all moving in a direction, he decided, making a pattern.** And he had to know where it was all leading. If he went home now, he'd never know. It was all part of learning what it meant to live in a good way.

....

It was all moving in a direction, he decided, making a pattern. This was what he was supposed to do.

BEFORE YOU MOVE ON...

1. **Conflict** What would Cloyd have to sacrifice to help Walter?

2. **Plot** Reread page 211. Compare how Cloyd made the decision to live with Walter to how he made decisions in the rest of story.

LOOK AHEAD Read pages 214–220 to find out how Walter and Cloyd change.

*Walter and Cloyd live together at the farm.
Cloyd learns to fix the house and he decides
to give Walter a special gift.*

22

It was the second Saturday in November, and they were repairing the foundation under the house. They'd started the weekend before. The project wasn't Walter's idea; Cloyd had remembered him worrying about it during the summer and reminded him of it. Walter had to admit it was a bad situation and getting worse. Walls, roof, and all would start to **give before long**.

Walter still had the cast on his leg, and he knew he couldn't **negotiate** the basement stairs. Wrapped up in a blanket, he sat in a chair at the top of the landing, where he could see the boy down below. **He had to content himself with lending know-how and moral support.**

....

give before long fall down soon

negotiate walk down

**He had to content himself with lending know-how and
moral support.** All he could do was give Cloyd advice and
encouragement.

Cloyd was mixing concrete. He'd carried the hundred-pound bags of cement downstairs himself, as well as countless buckets of sand and gravel, and now he was making concrete. It was chilly in the basement, but as long as he was working, he was warm enough in his denim jacket. He was happy taking care of the old man. He'd grown so used to wandering alone in the canyons, wandering alone in the school corridors, **having his own private world**. Now he wasn't alone anymore.

Cloyd felt strong. He could do **whatever he set his mind to**. He was never going to give up—he had a life to live. "Maybe it's all you've got," the old man had said. "Might as well make the most of it."

If he ever had any children, he was going to care about them, the way Walter cared. If he ever had a son, he was going to name him Walter. The old man would be dead and buried by then, he realized. It wouldn't matter. He would show them Walter's picture, and one day he would take them up to the meadows of Pine River.

Cloyd checked the batch of concrete he was mixing. It was just about right. More water would weaken it. He hoped the weather would **give them a few days**. The snow

....

having his own private world being alone
whatever he set his mind to anything he wanted
give them a few days be nice so that they would have more time
with their work

from the October storm had thawed, leaving the ground unprotected. With the cold air moving in, he worried that the earth was freezing solid at this very moment. They needed the soil outside that broken wall to **have some give in it**, so there'd be room for the wall to move over. Cloyd had another reason, too, for hoping the ground would **keep** a few days and he could dig in it. Thinking about his secret reason made him feel good. He wished for a snowstorm that would blanket the ground and keep it warm. Maybe they'd get one—after breakfast he'd seen a thick layer of high clouds advance from the west and cover the sun. A good storm could be **on its way**. This time, Walter had said, the snow would stick, and winter would have come to stay.

Cloyd poured his concrete into the holes he had dug in the crawl space. Then he **troweled the new footers smooth**. The work went well, and he was pleased.

So was the old man. "Tomorrow we'll cut those railroad ties so's they fit between our concrete footers and that good wall. Then we'll build a framework between the two walls and jack it tight. With the railroad ties behind

....

have some give in it be soft

keep stay soft

on its way coming

troweled the new footers smooth made the concrete smooth and straight on top

it, you know that good wall ain't gonna give. That other'n's gonna have to move over where it belongs."

Cloyd **knew the plan by heart**. He was pleased that he understood it so well, pleased that he was learning so many new things. When they jacked the framework tight between the two walls, the bulging one would start to give. Every day when he came home from school, he'd go down in the basement and crank the jack a little more. The crack in the wall would close up. When the wall was straight-up-and-down again, they'd **simplify** the supports that held it.

It was lunchtime, and it was warm in the kitchen with the cookstove fire going. The old man was fixing sandwiches. Walter made up the grocery lists, and Cloyd did the shopping in town. Every few days he'd go to the store during the lunch break at school. He had some friends this year, and sometimes they went with him. The teachers let him keep the groceries in their lounge; they even had a refrigerator for the fresh things. Walter insisted on doing the cooking. Cloyd thought that was fine. The doctor had said Walter needed to be doing

....

knew the plan by heart understood what he needed to do
simplify take away some of

things, **only nothing strenuous**.

On the kitchen table, with Walter's help, Cloyd struggled at writing a letter to his sister and his grandmother. He told them about Walter, how they'd gone into the mountains, that Walter had been hurt, that he was taking care of Walter until he got stronger. He knew Susan James had made sure they'd heard all those things, but he wanted to tell them himself. "I like the mountains, but I miss the desert," he wrote. "It's getting cold here now. Already it snowed once. I feed the horses in the morning, two bales of hay. Pretty soon I will shovel snow off the pond and chop a hole for them to drink. Blueboy is my favorite. He's strong and smart. When I come home, Walter is going to bring Blueboy, too. He's mine to keep."

For dessert they had doughnuts, the store-bought kind caked with powdered sugar. The old man broke one of his long-standing rules by suggesting they eat them in the parlor, where unavoidably the powdered sugar fell to the carpet. "**Blends right in**," Walter chuckled. "Reminds me of a joke I'll bet you'd like."

The trace of a smile crossed Cloyd's face. "Oh?" he

....

only nothing strenuous but nothing too hard
Blends right in You can't see the white sugar on the white carpet

said, **anticipating one of the old man's tall tales**.

"This fellow was feeding doughnuts to his horse. Another fellow asks him **what for**. The first fellow says, 'To find out how many he'd eat before he asked for a cup of coffee'."

Cloyd flashed a wide smile, and his round face shone like the sun. The old man was holding his breath, his head **bobbing** up and down, cheeks puffed out, lips drawn tight. Cloyd began to laugh, Walter's breath exploded, and then the old man was laughing, too, until his ears turned red.

They heard a vehicle pull up outside, and both went to the window to see. A young man was getting out of a white pickup with big red letters on the side.

"Durango Hardware and Nursery," Walter said. "Must be lost." The old man took his jacket from the peg in the mudroom and went outside to see if he could give directions.

The driver had taken off the glove on his right hand to turn the pages of his order book. "Here's your receipt," he said mechanically. He tore out a small yellow page and

....

anticipating one of the old man's tall tales getting ready to hear Walter's joke

what for why

bobbing moving

handed it to the old man. "The **seedlings** are in the back of the truck."

"Seedlings?" Walter protested.

"All paid for. Twenty-two peach trees. You are Cloyd Atcitty, aren't you?" the young man asked, reaching for his back pocket. "The manager gave me this map."

Cloyd stepped up. "I'm Cloyd Atcitty," he said. "I bought them. It was a surprise," he explained, motioning toward the old man with his lips.

For an instant, **Walter's eyes found Cloyd's**. The boy was glowing with pleasure.

"I never heard of anybody growing peaches around here," the driver offered skeptically. "Too cold, isn't it?"

"I suppose it is. . . ." Walter admitted, winking at Cloyd. "But **we'll sure give it a try**."

....

seedlings young trees

Walter's eyes found Cloyd's Walter and Cloyd looked at each other

we'll sure give it a try we will try to grow them

BEFORE YOU MOVE ON...

1. **Conclusions** How did the relationship between Cloyd and Walter change?

2. **Inference** Why did Cloyd buy Walter the seedlings? What did he want to tell Walter?